THE ADVENTURES OF NO H TRYING

A STRANGE ALLIANCE

Robert Villier

Book One
Trilogy

PREFACE

My trilogy originated as unfinished bedtime stories for my daughter Charlotte. Many years later they have finally been committed to paper after she insisted I finish them, if only for her son and my grandson Harrison.

There is no apology for the use of adult language, as it may serve to possibly engage and amuse all ages. Included are a number of snippets of factual information (knowledge is never wasted) that have been woven into the thread of the three stories, embroidered with an appliqué of fact, fiction and fantasy – just for fun.

The author

DEDICATION

This trilogy is for

my grandson and my hero

Harrison George Cwajna

APPRECIATION

My loving thanks goes to my ever supportive wife Sandra — whose illustrations may help with your imagination, to Charlotte for making the books possible and Harrison who continues to be my motivator.

Finally, my appreciation and acknowledgement goes to a good friend Helen. Her relentless encouragement, unstinting efforts and guidance helped shape all three stories - hopefully into readable and coherent prose. Eventually, after countless iterations, numerous ink cartridges and at least one rain forest — we made it, and are *still* the best of friends!

Contents

Chapter One
Two missing

The sun had gone well past its highest point and had been making its daily descent through a cloudless blue sky for some hours. It was late afternoon in the African savannahs, still pleasantly warm, the day having thankfully lost its torrid intensity of heat. Now was probably the best time of the day; second only to when the sun rose, which gave birth to each new morning and provided heat and energy to both people and animals.

It was like any other twenty-four hours in the grasslands of this hot continent, as two different groups went about their daily business. Paradoxically, there was a striking similarity between them, although they were very different! This very difference between our two groups now becomes most apparent.

The first group consisted of about forty of the largest-living-land-animals-on-the-planet: elephants. They walked at a slow and measured pace, lumbering along in virtually single file, large, medium and small in size, with a few stragglers wandering off from the straight line formation.

They were interspersed with nine much smaller and newer members, some of which were clearly having difficulty keeping up and staying in their usual positions. An occasional larger trunk would sometimes guide or swipe them back into line. Bringing up the rear was a nine-month old baby elephant, acting as 'tail-end Charlie.'

The other group that was not very far from the elephants was much smaller in size – in all respects. It was a hunting party of eight tribesmen – seven adults and one boy, also proceeding in single file. They were all bare-footed, wearing long bright red sarongs which hung from their waists. In their hands they carried their trusty weapons – a spear and shield.

They were split in the middle by a horizontal pole from which hung their hunting trophy – a dead impala. They walked on singing their favourite songs, as they did after every successful hunt. Bringing up the rear was a nine-year old boy, also acting as 'tail-end Charlie'!

As the two groups – one of elephants and one of tribesmen - went on their separate ways, no one could possibly have foreseen what fate had in store for them. A minor mishap, a sheer fluke and a wonderful chance encounter, were soon to have the most profound effect on their lives and indeed on those of many others.

It was an ordinary day in the African grasslands, with nothing to distinguish it from the thousands of others that had gone before. The elephants and tribesmen continued to go about their tasks, each unaware of the other's existence. For the time being, however, they were oblivious to what the future had in store for them all.

—∞—

The rear baby elephant interrupted the tedium of yet another boring walk, by playing his own private games, always with a mischievous twinkle in his eye whenever he could. This may be hide-and-seek with the other youngsters, or weaving through the many older and much larger legs – it passed the time. Sometimes it involved running off from the rest of the herd and hiding. But this latest escapade and unplanned detour was to be his undoing. It may have been that the other elephants had seen this particular baby elephant's diversionary tactics so many times, that they simply ignored him - accustomed to his comings and goings.

He thought he spotted some movement in the nearby undergrowth, and wandered off to investigate. Nothing was found, but he did find a lush oasis of succulent leaves and berries. This unexpected surprise banquet was too good to be missed; unfortunately he was not too good to be missed! For some unknown reason, his mother did not notice his departure, probably because it was becoming an all too common occurrence.

By the time the youngster looked up from his feast, the herd was nowhere to be seen. It had plodded on unaware that tail-end Charlie was missing! The lost elephant decided, quite logically, that the herd would eventually realize he was missing and come back for him. At least that was his rationale and what he hoped would happen! He reasoned that it would be prudent to stay where he was, and therefore, why not take advantage of the fresh food on offer? Best make use of the time available.

—∞—

The group of tribesmen were making good progress on their journey home after a successful day with their spears. This was evident from the suspended dead animal - the impala would provide food for the village for days ahead. They were flushed with success and pleased that the heat of the day had gone.

The bare-foot boy in the rear was slight in stature and clad only in a sarong of many colours and sporting a well-worn and battered straw hat. Just then, a strong gust of wind lifted the boy's straw boater clear off his head, and it went bouncing and gambolling away at a pace. He turned and gave immediate chase - he did not want to lose his beloved hat at any cost. He wasn't unduly concerned and was confident that with his speedy legs he would easily retrieve it, and quickly regain his place at the end of the file of hunters, but he achieved neither.

Sometimes luck can play cruel tricks, and the boy's hat made its way into the middle of a small but deep waterhole. Surrounding the water, in all directions, and as far as the eye could see there was flat unbroken grassland. But somehow his hat had managed to find its way to the only inaccessible resting place for kilometres around.

In the meantime, the seven tribesmen walked on and continued to sing merrily; knowing that they were well on their way home after a successful hunt, unaware their tail-end Charlie was missing!

The lost boy had not expected to be separated from his fellow hunters and the unfortunate mishap with his hat was unforeseen. But he couldn't just give up and declare his hat lost, not without at least having made some effort to get it back. He was confident that his fellow hunters would soon come looking for him. Best he use the waiting time trying to retrieve his most treasured possession – his hat.

The matriarch – the leader of the herd of elephants, and the baby elephant's mother were still unaware that they had a missing member and the matriarch led her group onwards.

The tribesmen were still unaware that they had a missing member, and they moved onwards.

But a nine-month old baby elephant and a nine-year old boy were missing.

—∞—

Chapter Two
Such unusual names

In the meantime, the baby elephant wandered into a clearing to find a sad young boy sitting beside a water hole. The boy looked glum, his chin resting in his propped hands, staring out at his beloved straw boater hat which bobbed out of reach in dark deep water. It looked like a yellow raft floating serenely, proudly boasting a purple ribbon, which fluttered in the occasional breeze.

With the depth of water unknown, the boy dared not venture in, as he could not swim. All he could do was lie flat on his stomach and lean out as far as he could. He splashed the water with his hands hoping it would persuade the straw hat to alter course and come inshore. It was to no avail; the more he tried the more the hat remained stubbornly out of arms reach.

The boy looked up, startled by the sudden appearance of this sizeable strange grey newcomer, and said, without really thinking,

"Oh you frightened me!" The baby elephant immediately said,

"Sorry, I didn't mean to alarm you, but I seem to have got myself lost!" The boy looked up, wide-eyed and spluttered,

"You *spoke* to me, and you completely understood what I said to you; but you're an elephant, how is this possible?" The elephant replied embarrassed,

"I suppose I am rather unusual and it is a rare ability that I have. In fact, you are the first person I've been able to talk to."

The boy shook his head, dumbfounded, trying to convince himself that the sun had not affected him, or that he was hallucinating or imagining it. Here was an elephant speaking in his own language, would his tribe believe him?

The elephant slowly walked closer to the stunned boy, and asked,

"Why are you looking so despondent?" (*Such a long word for an elephant*). "Are you lost too?" The boy pointed to the island of reeds saying,

"My treasured possession —my hat, is over there. It's just my rotten luck, and yes — I'm lost too!" The elephant summed up their predicaments quite succinctly,

"We're both lost, of that there is no question, and I suspect on balance, we were both to blame. I got distracted and separated from my herd and presumably you got distracted by the loss of your hat." The boy nodded his whole-hearted agreement.

"However, we need to find our families as soon as we can, after we have tried to retrieve your hat. I can see how much it means to you." Again the boy nodded gratefully, at the same time still trying to take in the incredible fact, that he and a baby elephant were talking and understanding each other!

He thought to himself, 'Fate might have played an unfair trick on me regarding my hat, but it has more than compensated for it with the stroke of exceptional good fortune of meeting a talking elephant.'

Without further ado, they slowly circumnavigated *(such a long word even for a nine-year old boy)* the water hole, looking to see what options there were for retrieving the hat. Alas, no obvious course of action presented itself. The elephant then admitted that the water looked rather deep.

"I've only wallowed in shallow water and haven't been out of my depth before. Perhaps if I pick a bulrush, I could hold it with my trunk and use it as an extended brown poker and reach it that way. Let's give it a go, it's worth a try!"

This is exactly what he tried; he wrenched one of the tallest bulrushes out of its bed of reeds, and used it as a trunk-come-fishing rod. He tried and tried, but the bulrush kept splashing into the water, fractionally short of the yellow raft, that had now defiantly lodged in a thick clump of reeds. The hat's purple band looked like a ship's ensign.

In the end, the boy reluctantly had to declare,

"It's no good my dear friend, you've tried so hard, indeed you've kept on trying – quite beyond the call of duty! I can't ask anymore of you. We really do need to turn our attention to the more important and pressing matter of finding our families."

In the space of a few minutes the young boy had already subconsciously accepted that he could indeed communicate with the elephant! At the same time the elephant had also realized that he and the boy were now on speaking terms – so to speak! He had always thought he possessed this unique but latent talent but now he'd proven it to be true.

The elephant finally had to admit defeat. The straw boater definitely had a mind of its own, floating elusively out of reach, with seemingly no intention whatsoever of surrendering its new found freedom. All this open space and the hat had to find the one and only water hole!

This unusual couple then moved away from the water hole, trying to work out which way the herd and the hunters had gone. It didn't take them long to realize that both groups had disappeared – completely! By now the sun was low, as were their spirits, and the daylight had become dusk. It was amazing how quickly night replaced day. The sky to the west was a breath-taking vision of oranges and reds, as the fiery ball of the sun rapidly disappeared below the horizon. But our friends were not really in the right mood to appreciate nature's magnificence.

The boy involuntarily shivered; the drop in temperature was sudden and noticeable to him, but probably not to the elephant.

The baby elephant looked at the young boy and said,

"Sorry about your hat, I really thought we would be able to get it back. It seems that you have lost your hat but found a friend; I'm going to call you No Hat!" The boy replied,

"You couldn't retrieve my hat for me, but you really did keep on trying; I'm going to call you Keep Trying!"

—∞—

That is the story of how our two heroes met – purely by chance, possessing a unique ability to talk and giving each other such unusual names. If you told anyone such a story, they would simply not believe you – but it was true.

Here they were, a baby elephant and a young African boy talking and relating to each other and, despite the disparity of ages, thinking and acting as if they were on the same wave-length: it is too far-fetched for words.

What was not so far-fetched however, was the stark reality that they were very much alone and they were not sure whether they liked it or not! Little did they know, as they stood side by side in the enveloping darkness, out in the grasslands of Africa, what fate had in store for our two lost friends. No Hat shuddered again, this time he didn't know if it was because of the approaching darkness, the cold, or if he was frightened. What he did know was that he was really relieved that he was lost but not entirely on his own. Unbeknown to No Hat and Keep Trying, this was the first of many adventures they were to share together.

—∞—

Chapter Three
Lost together

By now the sun had completely gone, replaced by the overcoat of night. They both knew it was too late and too dark to start searching for their families. With few options, No Hat and Keep Trying snuggled up next to each other on the ground not far from the water hole.

They were both lost but they had found a new friend. At least for the time being, it was better for both of them to be together. Far away the hunters had reached their village but there were one short. The herd of elephants had also plodded on, also one short. Keep Trying took the kind and unusual step of lying down besides No Hat, to give him comfort and warmth. This was a really thoughtful thing to do because he didn't really want to lie down at all. Elephants only sleep about two hours each night and rarely lie down, and if they do it's for a very good reason – normally a problem.

Although in the case of baby elephants that's not strictly true! It takes time for these rather large infants to become sure of foot. It is not uncommon to see youngsters slipping, sliding and falling all over the place – all part of the learning curve of growing up. At the water holes it was great fun to splash and roll over, but on the hard sloping grounds it was still quite painful. Keep Trying would have much preferred to remain standing and partake of a light overnight snack. This, however, was an exceptional situation and he was after all, an exceptional elephant!

Keep Trying didn't feel the cold - he was too thick-skinned. Like all elephants, his skin was extremely tough – an amazing two and a half centimetres thick. Yet despite this, Keep Trying, like all elephants, was extremely susceptible to sunburn. Although his skin was tough, it was also extremely sensitive.

This was a good excuse and an important reason for wallowing. It was an ideal setting for socializing with the other young elephants and the mud acted as a sunscreen and protected his skin from the harsh ultraviolet radiation from the sun. It also helped him get rid of insect bites and prevented the loss of moisture, which could cause serious damage. He soon discovered that he could effectively use his trunk as a snorkel. Blowing water and soil on to his body was not just fun, even though it was one of his favourite pastimes, it also helped to dry his body and bake on a new protective coat.

His only complaint was that the interval between these glorious wallowing sessions was far too long!

No Hat lay with Keep Trying's trunk wrapped around him, with his large ear acting as a small blanket. No Hat arranged his sarong to cover as much of his cold body as possible. As he lay shivering next to one of the largest-living- land-animals-on-the-planet, he reflected on what had happened to him in such a short space of time. One minute he had been a fascinated observer at a successful hunt, the next minute he was happily singing along with the rest of the hunters, the next minute he'd lost his much-treasured hat and the next minute he was completely lost.

Then out of the blue, he had met and established a strange alliance with an animal that could talk! Hitherto, he would have considered elephants to be dangerous and to be kept at arms' length. Now here he was, snuggled up next to one, trying desperately to keep within arms' length. It was indeed a funny old world he concluded, as he nestled up close to his new large bed mate, who was far from cuddly!

Life for No Hat was busy, exciting and fun, as it was for all the children in his village. He was nine years of age, with not enough hours in the day. His time was shared between helping his father to farm their small plot of land, attending school, being a member of occasional hunting parties, helping his mother with chores and playing with his peers. His parents were simple, hardworking people, and he was their only child, and very much their pride and joy. The inside of their hut was furnished with two blankets. They didn't have anything else. There was a small assortment of pots and pans outside the hut and an enclosed area for chickens. Yet, for their few possessions, he and his family were rich in many other ways and were happy and content with their lifestyle.

Both of his grandparents were now dead, but they had lived long enough to enjoy his company and early years. His grandparents hut now stood derelict nearby. The thatch had long gone; all that remained was a number of irregular wooden poles still resembling the shape of a hut but only just. Life for No Hat was good and he had no complaints, until now, when he'd got himself lost!

—∞—

They both got through the night, although it was long and uncomfortable, and cold for No Hat, but at least they were together! The sun rose slowly, as did No Hat. Shivering and feeling stiff, he stretched his arms out and ran on the spot to get his circulation moving.

Keep Trying was content with a few twirls of his trunk and was unaffected by the low temperature, perhaps his large thick grey overcoat had something to do with it. No Hat quivered,

"We need to find our families, where do we start?" Keep Trying waved his trunk in agreement adding,

"Yes, and as quickly as we can, before it's too late, or worse still - other animals find us!" Before they set off, they agreed to have one last attempt to rescue No Hat's yellow hat.

It was evident that during the night the hat had made no attempt to free itself from the clump of reeds in which it was securely moored. Keep Trying picked a bulrush which provided a further metre to his, it has to be said, rather short trunk. He tried to flick the hat, but alas, his efforts were to no avail and No Hat resigned himself to being hatless. Keep Trying had been as good as his word and his name - he did keep trying.

They bid farewell to No Hat's hat; which seemed both determined and destined to be 'lost at sea', and set off and away from the water hole. By now the tracks left by the herd of elephants and the hunters had grown faint and cold and it was quite apparent that they had no idea where they were. That's the problem with being young and carefree, you just tag on behind and let others lead the way.

No Hat and Keep Trying hadn't an inkling in which direction they should be heading. Yet, sometime during the night they had drawn comfort, strength and courage from each other. For sure, they must have had a kind guardian angel looking after them, as this invisible bond was to hold them in good stead for this and subsequent adventures.

—∞—

Chapter Four
A feathered friend

It was indeed a bizarre situation in which they both found themselves. Keep Trying had never in his short life of nine months, been in contact with any other type of animal let alone a human being. His life revolved completely around his herd, his mother and his food. This was by far the longest he had ever gone without a regular feed of milk, normally two litres at a time from his mother. Now he had a new friend whom he could communicate with.

No Hat was in much the same position. His short life of nine years had revolved around his family, friends and tribe. In this time he had been taught to be very wary of the largest living land animals on the planet. History and experience had shown how dangerous and destructive elephants could be. Now they were together, both comfortable and unafraid of each other, indeed they had already established a distinct and intuitive rapport and quite miraculously they could talk to each other fluently!

Keep Trying was the first to offer No Hat a lift,

"Four legs are better than two," he said laughing. Then, with the help of his trunk and raised foreleg, No Hat quickly climbed up and found himself sitting astride Keep Trying's back.

With his sarong pulled up high, his bare legs were only just long enough for him to sit safely and comfortably. Keep Trying's skin was tough, his short bristly hairs coarse to his touch – just like sandpaper! No Hat said,

"I'm certainly going to get very sore legs if I'm up here for long; but I'm not going to look a gift horse (or an elephant) in the mouth!'

It was at this moment that the third member of this strange party arrived. A beautiful yellow-billed oxpecker bird landed gently behind No Hat on the rump of Keep Trying. The oxpecker was about nine inches in height and a light brown in colour. He had a thick flat yellow beak with a red tip, bright red eyes which were surrounded by two distinctive yellow rings, a stiff tail, short legs and sharp claws.

His normal working day consisted of clinging to cattle, big-game or even impalas, (but not normally on elephants) living off the millions of unseen ticks and insects that permanently resided in the many crevices of their thick hides.

Keep Trying was an exception to this and completely relaxed at having the bird on his rump. One of the oxpeckers tricks was to hiss to alert his host to any possible threats or danger, and in this way paid for his ride! This skill, peculiar only to the oxpecker, would be put to good use in the time ahead. The bird was quite unafraid of the added presence of No Hat and decided that he enjoyed the company and that it made a pleasant change from flying everywhere.

No Hat asked Keep Trying, "Do you mind him joining us?"

"Not at all" Keep Trying replied.

"I've got used to the daily visitations of the oxpecker," he philosophically added,

"We all have our part to play!"

This was a very profound thing to say, especially by a baby elephant. He was of course a very exceptional elephant, as we know!

In the meantime, our feathered friend had already taken it for granted that there would be no objections to his joining the party. Looking at them, they certainly made an unusual team trio: an elephant, a boy and a bird.

The three set off on their search, even though the oxpecker didn't yet know what they were searching for because he could not talk to his two fellow travellers. He did not possess any special powers, other than being able to fly – which I suppose is rather special!

He could, however, listen to No Hat and Keep Trying talking to each other. As they walked, they talked non-stop and asked each other so many questions.

"How many are there in your village?"

"How many are there in your herd?"

"How old are you?"

"Where were you born?" and

"What do you want to do when you grow up?"

They had become very talkative friends in such a short space of time. The oxpecker began to appreciate their plight and their pressing mission. Initially he thought he would just go along for the ride, but now he could see that they were both feeling alone and afraid. The oxpecker decided, there and then, that he had to think of a way of helping them, but how? He returned to his scavenging, thinking of how he could be of assistance.

—∞—

No Hat had a feeling that when they strayed from their families, both herd and men were heading in roughly the same direction. It would, therefore, be sensible to go the same way and try to pick up the trails. A heap of elephant droppings – dung - provided the first and only indication of which way to go. The golden heaps had dried in the sun, showing that the herd had passed this way some time before.

Keep Trying set off at a gentle plod, the only speed he seemed to have, with No Hat sitting, it has to be said, rather uncomfortably onboard, and the oxpecker implacably perched at the rear, conscientiously continuing with his scavenging chores. It took No Hat quite a while to get used to riding on Keep Trying's back and the inside of his thighs were already chaffed, but it was still preferable to walking!

It is probably obvious, but No Hat and Keep Trying hoped desperately that they were indeed on the right track. What if they were heading in completely the wrong direction? It didn't bear thinking about! The drying heaps of dung were their only clue. Keep Trying logically pointed out,

"Best we follow these little signposts and put any thoughts of being on the wrong track completely out of our minds."

The slight and apprehensive boy, recently named No Hat, nodded; it was exactly the sensible assurance he needed at that moment in time. He thought of the dead impala and reminded himself that it was not only tribesmen who went hunting. There would be plenty of other large animals also out hunting, on the prowl and looking for food.

Meanwhile, the yellow-billed oxpecker had firmly established himself as the third member of the team. Between nibbles, the assured and precocious bird made an occasional reconnaissance flight in search of both men and elephants. So far none of his flights had been fruitful; but not to worry, there would be other opportunities – he hoped. He decided that he would have to widen his aeronautical search area tomorrow; he could *tell* that No Hat and Keep Trying were really worried.

He was determined to pay his way to these very likeable, but concerned youngsters.

Many kilometres away the reaction of the herd's matriarch and the villager's chieftain was quite different.

Keep Trying's mother had been advised by the matriarch that the herd would remain in the same area for the next two to three days, in the hope that the missing youngster would find his own way back. Only then would the herd retrace its steps for the lost baby elephant.

No Hat's parents had no problem in convincing the chieftain that an immediate search party was the right course of action. There was no shortage of volunteers from the fastest and fittest hunters, and they had set off at first light the following morning. Most worryingly they had returned with still no sighting of their lost nine-year old boy.

—∞—

Chapter Five
The river crossing

No Hat and Keep Trying heard the thunderous roar of the waterfall long before it or the river came into view. As they nervously approached the fast running river, clearly in full flow, both were filled with alarm at the dangers that immediately confronted them.

Now they could see the waterfall! It was only two hundred paces downstream, tossing and hurling huge clouds of spray high into the sky. The recent rains had greatly swollen the river and it was at least fifty or so metres wide — a formidable obstacle for our two heroes to overcome if they were to find their families. They had seen further dung droppings on the other bank — hence the need to cross.

They knew that to try and cross anywhere near that raging torrent would be madness and would end in certain disaster. No Hat dismounted and threw a small twig into the rushing water; within seconds it had disappeared from sight into the white wall of spray. Keep Trying was clearly agitated and rocked from side to side, waving his trunk high in the air.

He turned to No Hat and said,

"I'm not sure I can swim in such a fast running river, let's go upstream and see if we can find a calmer stretch of water – please!" No Hat didn't need much encouragement or persuading and nodded his whole-hearted agreement!

The oxpecker appreciated the dilemma and flew off high into the air. Circulating overhead he had the perfect bird's eye view of the surrounding area. The river was indeed running extremely fast, carrying many branches, logs and other fallen debris into the foaming mass of bubbling water.

The waterfall displayed its awesome power as thousands of tons of water continuously plunged downwards for some eighty metres, crashing to the river's lower level. This whole spectacle was framed in a permanent rainbow, in one of nature's artistic touches of brilliance and beauty.

At this time, our two heroes didn't fully appreciate the magnificence of the sight before them. The oxpecker was amazed at how quickly the river below the waterfall became calm again before continuing on its journey.

The sandy river banks provided a favourite place for many crocodiles to bask in the sun. Crocodiles congregate in freshwater habitats of rivers, lakes and wetlands. They are ambush hunters, waiting for fish or land animals to come close and then they rush to attack.

They have obviously perfected their technique, as they have been around for about 55 million years! Their streamlined bodies allow them to be successful predators - they can swim and move very swiftly, even out of water. Since they feed by grabbing onto their prey, they have evolved very sharp teeth for tearing and holding onto flesh, and powerful muscles to close their jaws and hold them shut. These jaws bite down with immense force; they have by far the strongest bite of any animal. They are not creatures that No Hat or Keep Trying wanted to be anywhere near.

From his high aerial vantage point, the oxpecker could see a possible crossing point someway up river, above the waterfall, near to a bend. It was still wide and it would not be easy, but it did at least offer them a better chance of crossing successfully.

He landed back on Keep Trying's grey rump and guided him with a series of chirrups and hisses, to a spot where the bank sloped gently down to the water's edge.

Thankfully, the river was not running so fast – or so they thought. No Hat and Keep Trying took a deep breath, and bravely wished each other 'good luck for a safe crossing and a happy landing.' This was a plucky display of courage from our two youngsters, with no help available for many miles apart from the oxpecker – and the odd crocodile or two!

No Hat held tightly on to Keep Trying's ears, as the baby elephant slid gently and tentatively into the water - immediately out of his depth. It was not unlike the launching of a ship, as it slides down the slipway and into the water, then – floating.

No Hat knew that if he were to fall off, he would instantly be swept down river and over the bellowing waterfall. It would be farewell to No Hat! Both were surprised by how cold the water was and it took their breath away for a few seconds.

The oxpecker was the only member of the trio to remain calm and unflustered by the launch as he sat on Keep Trying's rump. Keep Trying was frightened, he had never been in a river before, let alone a fast moving one, and we must not forget that he was still less than a year old!

He instinctively began moving his legs under the water and they all moved forward. No Hat held on with all his strength, his feet and lower legs trailing under the surface.

As they got further out into the river, it became clear that they were being carried downstream by the current, and ever closer to the waterfall. No Hat was now visibly scared, with wide eyes and a look of alarm on his face. He dug his legs into Keep Trying's flanks, pointing frantically at the plumes of spray getting closer and closer. Keep Trying shouted back, trying to make his voice heard above the noise of the thundering roar,

"Don't panic just hold on tight, I won't let you down, we're going to make it." Then with a sustained super-elephant effort, he increased the tempo of his underwater paddling, as the far bank grew encouragingly nearer.

It was an exhausted baby elephant and a shaking and trembling boy that clambered and slithered up the slippery bank and onto the safety of dry land. The oxpecker must have flown away sometime during the crossing. Both were exhausted and drained by their ordeal.

Keep Trying moved away from the edge of the river and stood quite still, clearly trying to recover his composure, inwardly shaken by his first introduction to deep water and the tremendous effort required to cross the river. He had been acutely aware of his frightened friend and passenger, urging him on. There was *no way* he would have let him down.

No Hat lay panting on the ground, the exertions of holding onto Keep Trying and the fear of the fast running river carrying them away and over the thundering waterfall, showing in his shaking body. He propped himself up on one elbow to reassure himself that Keep Trying – his brave and trusted companion - was indeed all right. The oxpecker returned; he obviously did not like having his feathers splashed. Two long and sleek-looking logs, with eyes and teeth, slithered into the water - crocodiles! Keep Trying and No Hat had made it! They were safe; it had been a Herculean achievement by our heroes.

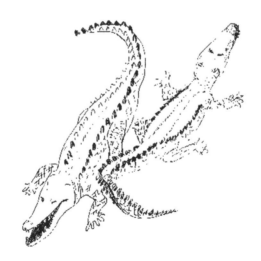

Chapter Six
Ivory poachers

The drama and scares of the river ordeal were now behind them. No Hat looked in disbelief at the wide expanse of racing waters and thought,

'Did we really cross all *that?*' Keep Trying, reading his mind cracked a joke saying,

"We should be able to swim, after all, we do have trunks!" No Hat smiled at his friend with warm affection and admiration, praising him for his courage, strength and sense of humour in the face of such adversity. Keep Trying was quite embarrassed by his partner's accolades. The oxpecker looked sartorially elegant, still trying to work out how he could help his two intrepid companions.

When they had fully recovered they set off again, as the sun climbed higher in the sky. The top of No Hat's head was hot to the touch; how he wished he still had his beloved hat. Luckily the wind was getting up and this provided some welcome respite from the scorching heat, although the increasing power of the wind made it difficult even for the unflappable oxpecker to hold on.

No Hat also found it a struggle to keep his balance on Keep Trying's back. His mind went back to seeing those crocodiles and unconsciously he trembled. If they had seen the crocodiles before they entered the water, what then? Somewhere an ancestral spirit was looking after the baby elephant and young boy - the oxpecker seemed to be looking after himself very well!

—∞—

They had not travelled far when they heard the sound of gunfire and men shouting. The gunfire was a salvo of large bangs, not unlike the sound of the drums playing in the village on special occasions. But whereas the sound of drums was a happy sound, that of shooting normally meant killing and destruction. Gunfire meant hunters and hunters meant ivory poachers. The deplorable practise of poaching elephant tusks had been outlawed many years ago but this served only to intensify the many illegal poachers, brought on by the incessant supply and demand.

The greed of men was all too evident, with no shortage of hunters prepared to kill the largest-living-land-animals-on-the-planet and smuggle ivory to all parts of the world, and plenty of dealers being more than willing to take it.

Ivory is hard and smooth, like teeth, and a creamy yellow in colour. This makes it an attractive and desirable material for ornamental carvings and jewellery. A single tusk is about two metres long and weighs approximately forty kilograms – about the same weight as No Hat! A single tusk could be sold for a considerable amount of money, probably thousands of pounds or dollars. This is why the poachers were prepared to track elephants for hundreds of kilometres, and kill them in their lucrative, illicit and evil quest for ivory. Later the ivory tusks would be sold and traded through unscrupulous merchants, of which there were far too many, all prepared to make money out of this murderous trade.

—∞—

Luckily, our trio spotted the ivory hunters before they were spotted. They hurriedly hid themselves in the safety of a dense area of undergrowth, hardly daring to breathe, and resolved not to let the poachers see or hear them. The noise of an approaching vehicle got louder and louder, then all of a sudden the hunters appeared – very close to them, much closer than they expected! Three men ran in front of a large open-topped lorry, in which there stood three mean-looking khaki-clad hunters, all armed with powerful rifles. With ammunition bands wrapped across their chests they made a sinister picture.

At the rear of the lorry there were at least eight long and freshly taken tusks propped up, all showing clear signs of blood at their serrated bases. Keep Trying's heart missed a beat; could these tusks possibly have been taken from his herd, family and friends? The hunters were dirty and had obviously been out poaching for many days - you could almost *smell* them! Was there no length that these terrible men wouldn't go to, in order to satisfy their evil lust for ivory and money?

—∞—

No Hat and Keep Trying kept perfectly still in the undergrowth. No Hat could almost read Keep Trying's mind with its anxious thoughts. The oxpecker seemed to appreciate the situation (*but please - tell me how!*). All three remained frightened, motionless until the lorry and men disappeared. It was the second time No Hat and Keep Trying felt scared and vulnerable that day. As luck would have it, the wind had grown in strength and they were suddenly in the middle of a full-scale sandstorm.

Visibility was soon down to less than a metre and it was hard for No Hat to see even his hand in front of his face, as sand was whipped up and hurled in every direction. Within minutes everything in sight was completely covered. No Hat and Keep Trying looked like two vague red shapes, with fine sharp particles of sand clinging to every exposed part of their bodies. No Hat dare not shout out for fear of being heard by the poachers, although they too must have been experiencing the same agonies and discomfort.

The oxpecker had wisely disappeared before the sandstorm arrived, perhaps finding protection in some tree nearby.

The poachers passed close by, far too close for comfort, with their heads and eyes shielded, looking firmly at either the ground in front of them or the lorry floor. The vehicle moved further and further away and their voices became fainter until they had gone.

No Hat and Keep Trying breathed an almost audible sigh of relief. That was indeed a very close call! The sandstorm cleared as quickly as it had begun. There was no sign of the poachers - thank goodness. No Hat dusted himself off; Keep Trying didn't seem to be all that bothered!

The oxpecker re-emerged from his secret hideout, looking immaculate, with not a feather out of place *(how did he do it?)*. The bird seemed to know exactly the right time to come and go!

No Hat turned to Keep Trying and tried to reassure him,
"I know what you're thinking, but those men have been out in the bush for weeks, and those tusks could have come from any herd. For the time being, you must try and put those terrible thoughts out of your mind."

Keep Trying nodded and looked very sad.
"I'll try," he promised,
"But it's easier said than done, when you've just seen tusks that have come from either your own or another herd!"

—∞—

Chapter Seven
The pit

Keep Trying made a conscious effort to try to cheer himself up and lighten the mood and turned to No Hat and the oxpecker, saying,

"Come on you two, climb onboard. It's time we were on our way, before the poachers decide to return." They had only travelled some fifty metres when they heard a shout, a cry for help, coming from close ahead.

It sounded like a man's voice but not in a language that No Hat recognized and it seemed to be coming from under the ground! Having already heard the sound of gunfire, they were understandably nervous and apprehensive as Keep Trying walked cautiously up to the edge of what was a very deep pit.

The large hole must have been dug and covered over by an earlier gang of poachers; the aim being that any unsuspecting elephant would fall into the trap. The doomed animal would then be unable to climb out or escape, and at the mercy of the hunters when they returned – which could be days or weeks, or even months.

During the sandstorm one of the poachers had fallen into the pit, without the others realizing and his cries for help were lost and carried away on the wind. The poacher-come-trapper was now trapped himself and unable to climb out of the man-made excavation with its deep and sheer sides. Fortunately for the poacher, the youth and innocence of No Hat and Keep Trying knew no malice and they only saw a person in need of help.

When they looked into the pit they saw an unattractive, khaki-clad apparition, with a large gold earring and a spotted red and white bandanna which held in place long lank and matted hair. His face was covered with a huge black bushy beard and his mouth displayed dirty decaying teeth. His ugly features were completed with a large slanting scar, going from the middle of his forehead across to the top of one eyebrow. He had a lethal high-velocity rifle slung across his sweat-stained shirt, and was covered from head to toe in sand.

He looked a fearsome sight as he shouted out in a language No Hat didn't understand, but the meaning was clear, 'Help, please get me out!'

No Hat gesticulated that he would try and help. He went with Keep Trying to look for some long and strong tendrils of vine to use as a make-shift rope. They soon found exactly what they were looking for. Keep Trying plucked a thick vine from the huge tree from which it hung, and dragged it to the edge of the deep pit. Both were careful not to venture too close to its steep edge, for fear of falling in.

No Hat, using simple hand signals, made it clear to the poacher that he should remove his rifle and leave it where it was - they would only be helping him out, not his 'killing machine!' Reluctantly and mumbling, the poacher laid his rifle on the ground as No Hat had directed. Keep Trying lowered the vine slowly down into the pit, with one end wrapped round and firmly held by his trunk.

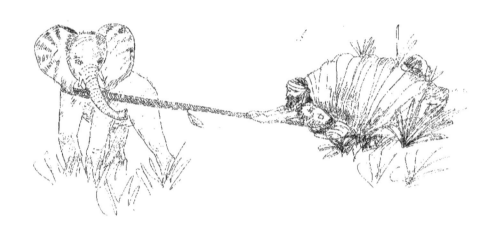

The poacher hurriedly wound the vine around his waist and held it firmly in his large and dirty hands. Keep Trying shuffled backwards, hauling the very lucky and bedraggled poacher up and out of the chamber of death. The poacher scrambled to his feet, and shouted his thanks. He grabbed and enveloped No Hat's hands in his own, shaking them vigorously, with obvious relief, even though No Hat had *not* offered his hands and was trying to keep his distance.

The poacher promised he would mend his ways. He told No Hat that he and this ingenious elephant had undoubtedly saved his life, babbling that he would have either starved to death or been attacked by other ferocious animals. Keep Trying, with the vision of the 'taken' tusks fresh in his mind could quite understandably have left him where they had found him!

The roles of the hunter and the hunted had definitely been reversed. The rescued hunter vowed that he would use this frightening and humbling experience to persuade his colleagues that elephants were to be respected and not chased and slaughtered for their ivory. He again uttered his disingenuous thanks and ran off in the direction of his fellow assassins.

No Hat and Keep Trying were not at all convinced by his pledges and didn't believe a single word he said – not for one moment! They knew that greed would prevail and that he and other gangs would continue with their same evil tricks.

His rifle remains at the bottom of the pit, even to this day.

Chapter Eight
Olympian dream

After their frightening ordeal and good deed, No Hat and Keep Trying needed something to eat. Keep Trying believed that he always needed something to eat, and was more than happy with the surrounding abundance of vegetation. The sand now camouflaged the leaves but the fine particles didn't seem to worry his digestive system one iota!

No Hat in the meantime had located a large bunch of bananas that were just turning yellow. This satisfied his immediate hunger, but he was thirsty, not having had a real drink since they crossed the river. The river crossing seemed such a long time ago.

He broke off another bunch of bananas and tied them up with a convenient nearby vine, laying them across Keep Trying's rump. They would provide sustenance at the end of the day. The oxpecker continued to feed off Keep Trying's plentiful supply of ticks. Again, the three set off in search of No Hat's and Keep Trying's families.

It had been a long and eventful day and they had both grown up a lot in the last twenty-four hours, although the oxpecker still seemed to be his regular and unruffled self.

It was nearly sunset when they fortuitously stumbled upon a much larger and welcoming water hole. They were both in need of liquid refreshment, admittedly in different quantities! At this point the oxpecker made a distinctive chirruping sound, as if telling his friends he was retiring to better accommodation for the night. Keep

Trying and No Hat confided and confessed that they had, in all honesty, completely forgotten all about their feathered friend!

At the same time Keep Trying excused himself from No Hat, saying, "It is time for a bath!"

No Hat quickly retrieved his bananas and sat watching his elephant friend enjoying a good splash and wallow. He let his mind escape into the world of make-believe, into some light-hearted fantasy to relieve the tension and stress of the dramas that they had been through, and would hopefully survive to tell the tale. No Hat closed his eyes, and his mind was the only spectator at his water hole.

The Olympic stadium was a scene teeming with animals of all shapes and sizes. The main arena was a cacophony of noises and smells, which invaded and excited No Hat's imaginary senses, his nostrils full of the pungent aromas of real animal dung.

Each type of animal was exhibiting their own particular skills and talents for either field or track events. The giraffes in the background looked on with lofty curiosity, watching the events taking place in front of them. Surely no one was going to take the high jump title away from them? The gymnasts in the trees swung effortlessly from branch to branch, looking just like monkeys; colourful parrots acted as time-keepers.

Impalas and gazelles competed with each other in the hop, step and jump, each trying to outdo the other in poise and elegance. The springboks stood waiting patiently *for the start of the high hurdles. Hippos and water buffalos rested in the water waiting for the tug-of-war.*

The zebras were already dressed for bed in their striped pyjamas, or did they always look like that? The baboons kept disturbing the flamingos, as they rehearsed their dancing steps. A cheetah hid in the bushes, waiting for the hundred metres dash, and the lion kings were there to umpire the whole event from a distance.

An elephant was in charge of the public address system – guess who! The crocodiles had been disqualified by the judges for bad behaviour – it was a dream, not a nightmare!

No Hat was brought out of his reverie and back to reality, as Keep Trying used his trunk as a watering can and showered him from head to toe - he was soaked! It was the first time that they had both really laughed!

Keep Trying had clearly enjoyed his bath. He had washed away the remaining particles of grit left from the sandstorm and went from being a dark red to a light grey.

No Hat then ventured to the water hole for a few sips of the dark murky liquid – better than nothing, he reassured himself.

Unfortunately, apart from Keep Trying, there were no signs of any other elephants, except large droppings of fairly warm dung, which meant they had been around, and not too long ago.

No Hat sat and watched Keep Trying enjoy one last final dip, after all he deserved it. Surprise, surprise, the oxpecker had vanished again!

The sun disappeared and the light of day was again replaced by eerie shadows, then the jet blackness of night. No Hat and Keep Trying were alone again, for yet more long, dark, cold hours together; the oxpecker safe and secure in some nearby tree – probably?

—∞—

This left our two heroes to bed down beside a large rock, with an enormous overhanging palm tree leaning over at a precarious angle, offering some protection. This was their second night together. Keep Trying thought to himself,

'I mustn't make a habit of all this lying down.' No Hat thought to himself,

'What a terrible mess I would be in if I didn't have Keep Trying as a companion and trusted friend.'

They both slept like logs after the exertions and dangers of their day together. Even Keep Trying had more than the normal two hours. Surely, herd and hunters would be looking for them by now? Our two heroes were now missing their families more than they dared or wished to let on to each other – like lions, they had their pride!!

—∞—

The matriarch and the chieftain had both reviewed their positions and decided differently on what to do.

'The herd was reluctantly returning to look for the lost elephant, not a practise they enjoyed or made a habit of,' the matriarch had informed Keep Trying's mother in no uncertain manner! They rarely returned because they had fairly well decimated the vegetation, and therefore meals would be light, but going back on this occasion was the only thing to do.

The chieftain, after a fruitless day of searching, had then widened their search to a full three hundred and sixty degrees. Small groups would search all four quadrants, camping out overnight if need be, rather than wasting time and energy to return to the village. He knew how far the returning hunting party had travelled from the actual 'impala killing ground', and was confident that they would find the boy.

His silent concern, which he did not share with the rest of the villagers, was whether the hunters would find the boy before other wild animals did. He was sure this had also crossed the minds of the others but no-one said it. No Hat's father was to lead the party, in the chieftain's favoured direction.

—∞—

Chapter Nine
One found

In the morning they all awoke at different times. Keep Trying had been up for some hours, after having an extended full breakfast and taking advantage of the empty swimming pool facilities. This helped to make up for the milk he craved.

The oxpecker had made an early start and carried out a few aerial missions, returning with nothing to report,   although he just thought he might have seen smoke. No Hat's alarm clock was the bitter African morning; he too was up bright and early, energetically trying to get warm (remember all he had on was a short sarong).

Then a wisp of smoke, barely discernible, appeared on the horizon, hopefully from the camp fire of a possible search party. Who else would be lighting fires in this part of the African savannah? It was the first sign of civilisation for three days. No Hat hurriedly and excitedly remounted Keep Trying and the coldness of the early start was instantly forgotten.

—∞—

Together they set off in the direction of the very faint taper of white smoke that rose into the air – it was a beacon of hope, but from afar, it resembled a candle.

No Hat's legs had now become fully acclimatised to riding on Keep Trying's back and were no longer sore, and he felt as one with his trusty companion. He turned his head and the oxpecker reappeared as if by magic. Keep Trying said,

"I think he sits in the trees waiting for us to move off." In fairness, the oxpecker had been looking, and he thought he'd seen the smoke too.

The hopeful trio set off towards the smoke that was now billowing and clearly visible. With urgency in Keep Trying's step, they soon approached the smoke, and could make out the shapes and colours of the tribesmen running towards them; to No Hat this was the most pleasing mass of colours imaginable.

His delight turned to elation when he saw his father leading the group of men, who were all wearing bright sarongs with an assortment of beaded necklaces and, without exception, carrying their own spear.

Their pleasure and relief were clear to see on all their faces. No Hat's father gave his son a rib-crushing hug, and at the same time gently scolded his 'pride and joy' for getting lost in the first place. It was obvious that he was just happy to have his son back, safe and sound.

Meanwhile, Keep Trying wandered off, no longer the centre of attraction — remember *he* was still lost!

—∞—

That evening, back in the village, around the chieftain's fire, No Hat recounted the story of meeting Keep Trying, and how incredible it was that they could speak and understand each other. The chieftain and No Hat's father nodded kindly, believing that the stress of the past three days had caught up with the boy. Best if they just humour him and go along with his story, he'll feel better after a good night's sleep!

This ability to communicate what he was talking about was too much for the elders to accept or comprehend - which is not all that surprising! No Hat went on to describe the loss of his beloved hat and the traumatic river crossing with the dreadful scare of seeing the deadly crocodiles nearby.

He recounted the stories of the fortuitous sandstorm and the horrible ivory poachers, and the one they had helped out of common decency. He also mentioned seeing elephant dung at the water hole, but he didn't think it prudent to mention his Olympian dream, having already noted the look of disbelief when he described a talking elephant!

Of course, the story would not have been complete without including reference to their faithful feathered friend – the oxpecker. Some of the elders nodded and smiled, they knew what clever little birds they were, this part of No Hat's story they did believe!

Keep Trying made the best of a bad deal and was well catered for - in fact he was quite spoilt. He was given masses of succulent leaves and water, plus the added bonus of some goat's milk, as suggested by No Hat's mother. He now ambled and foraged around the village perimeter. No Hat walked over to him and said,

"In the morning my family, friends and I will help find your herd – I promise. Try not to think about seeing those ivory hunters."

'Easier said than done,' Keep Trying thought to himself. He replied,

"Thank you No Hat," and for the first time in three days he realized how much he missed his own family.

No Hat enjoyed snuggling under his cosy blanket. Keep Trying was just relieved he didn't have to lie down for another night!

—∞—

Chapter Ten
All's well that ends well

No Hat was woken at daybreak by his father, who had already been up and about for some considerable time. The boy was still pleasantly 'coming to' and enjoying the novelty of waking up and not feeling as if he was freezing to death. He looked out from beneath his cosy blanket and saw frenetic activities in the village.

The chieftain had devised a plan of action and called the men together. Keep Trying stood a little way off, not appreciating that the commotion and effort was entirely on his behalf. No Hat was now up and dressed, eager to play his part in finding Keep Trying's herd, with his father having already been nominated to lead one of the searching groups.

The women and children were interested bystanders, as they were familiar with the men going off for days on end. Hadn't they just experienced the same thing when they were looking for No Hat? A couple of the women had jokingly remarked that it was nice to have the village to themselves for a change – but not too loudly.

A few goats and chickens wandered freely, searching for any morsels of food, oblivious to the hustle and bustle around them – not everyone was interested in finding a herd of elephants!

The chieftain explained that No Hat had seen elephant dung in the vicinity of the water hole. This suggested that the herd may have remained in the same area, especially as it offered the elephants an abundance of lush vegetation, still readily available to them.

The thirty tribesmen had been told by the chieftain to split up into three groups of ten, to make a three-pronged approach: one group to the left, one to the right and the third going straight ahead, to form a pincer movement in the direction of the water hole.

No Hat's father was again to lead the third group and his team knew that they had a strenuous and sustained run ahead of them. No Hat took his now familiar place onboard Keep Trying but the oxpecker was nowhere to be seen. The bird, determined to take part in the search, had decided to fly ahead and investigate.

The three groups set off, each chanting rhythmically, with Keep Trying valiantly struggling to keep up with the pace set by the men. No Hat was amazed at how strong and fit his father was - would he be like that one day?

An hour later the oxpecker returned flapping his wings violently and hissing at the approaching men - he was clearly trying to tell them something. He had flown ahead, and with the obvious advantage of height, could see further into the distance.

Below a slight rise, but still hidden to the tribesmen, he had spotted the herd. Cleverly he kept taking off and flying in the direction of the elephants, as if to say,

"Follow me, men!" The wise chieftain realized what the oxpecker was trying to tell them the way and altered the group's course. The men's bodies glistened, dripping with perspiration from running, but they showed no sign of tiredness. The oxpecker continued to hover in the direction of the herd.

Then, as they reached the high ground, grey shapes emerged in the distance. The oxpecker had again proved what a valuable member of the team he was. He and he alone, had found the herd. Suddenly, as they neared a dense area of undergrowth, the matriarch elephant appeared, closely followed by the rest of the herd. Keep Trying's mother trumpeted her recognition when she saw her baby, who in turn, squealed his delight.

His mother, out of sheer relief thought,

'I'll give him *such* a thick ear, when I catch up with him, for having worried us all out of our very thick skins!' But she wouldn't, she was far too happy to have her boy back, not that you could tell by her inscrutable look!

No Hat immediately realized what was happening and dismounted, giving Keep Trying a farewell pat of affection, with tears in his eyes, happy that he was also now reunited with his family. They had both found their families. But he was sad that their moment of parting had come, especially after all they had been through together. Keep Trying said,

"Thank you for everything, you have been really marvellous and I will always remember you as a brave, kind, thoughtful and true friend. It has been a privilege to be in your company." No Hat's face reddened as he smiled and reluctantly re-joined his father.

Some of the herd then surrounded Keep Trying and caressed him with their trunks affectionately. By now the other two groups of tribesmen had joined them, as they all stood in awe at the display taking place in front of them, an elephant and a boy talking to each other. The boy *had* been telling the truth after all!

The matriarch, a wise old elephant sensed the sadness of the occasion and moved amongst the other elephants in the herd, who took the hint and started to shuffle away.

Elephants don't cry, do they?

Keep Trying turned his head one last time to No Hat and waved his trunk in salute, then moved off with his greatly relieved mother and the rest of his herd.

The tribesmen cheered and raised their spears high into the air, as a mark of respect to the largest-living-land-animals-on-the-planet. The oxpecker did one final 'fly past' and then flew off to find new and alternative transport.

Résumé

This is how our two heroes met and gave each other such unusual names. It all started with the loss of the boy's beloved straw hat and resulted in their unusual, but in a funny way, appropriate names!   It was a formidable but strange alliance. The experiences they went through together were both frightening and exhilarating and above all character-forming. They were both to grow up and go their separate ways.

The oxpecker had been fun, good company, useful and had paid his fare in full. He remained in immaculate condition and was often to be seen on the backs' of other animals – with or without their permission!

Keep Trying grew up and became one of the most liked and trusted members of the herd, but was unable to use his unique talking talent with anyone else and it remained a secret to his herd. Sadly, but inevitably, there is not always a happy ending, and regrettably the largest living land animals on the planet would continue to be threatened by odious ivory hunters. They did, however, not have it all their own way, as it will subsequently be revealed.

No Hat was given another battered straw hat and compulsory swimming lessons. He would not be included in another hunting trip in the foreseeable future! No Hat would often recall the time when he was lost and alone in the African savannah apart from being with a talking elephant called Keep Trying. His father promised him that one day they would return to the infamous water hole, the catalyst that had brought about so many changes in their lives.

You would, however, be forgiven, for wrongly thinking this was the end of their story and adventures together, thanks to 'Miss Serendipity!' Fate had in mind a reunion for No Hat and Keep Trying. But for the time being, let's just say:

All's well that ends well

The End

THE ADVENTURES OF NO HAT AND KEEP TRYING

THE REUNION

Robert Villier

Book Two
Trilogy

Contents

Chapter One
The dam builders

It was almost four years since No Hat had said a sad farewell to Keep Trying and life had long since returned to normal. It was to change quite suddenly and dramatically, when one day the 'dam builders' arrived.

They explained to the chieftain, elders and other villagers that where the village now stood, would soon be underwater. The entire length of the valley in which they and generations of their ancestors had lived, would soon become part of a vast lake.

They were building a dam some miles downriver, and this would eventually stop and control the mighty waters that had wound its way through the African veldt for hundreds of years. They said it would turn the water into electricity.

This talk of 'hydro-electric' was too much for the tribesmen, this was *their* land, and they certainly hadn't seen any water! Surely the hot sun had turned the minds of these foreigners? Only one dam builder had a smattering of the tribal language, but he eventually succeeded in getting the full implications of the dam across to the tribesmen.

Now the sound of repeated explosions and blasting that they had been hearing for week after week began to make sense. The impact of this on the tribal community was devastating - not only for the thousands of tribesmen, but also for the many thousands of animals that lived in the valley.

What would happen to them and where would they all go? It was true the chieftain had been given prior warning of the dam by the dam builders many years ago, but he had decided not to share such bad news with his tribe. No Hat had also heard murmurings by some of his school friends, of these strange stories of blocking the river, but he had not taken them seriously.

The very idea was far too incredible a tale to take back to the village, but now it seemed it was true! Understandably, to the older folks it was totally beyond their comprehension and so they chose to blot out the very idea. The chieftain listened politely and patiently until the dam builders had finished articulating the merits of the dam, and the prosperity and the power it would bring.

The chieftain caustically pointed out that,

"*They* will be gaining this prosperity and *we* the tribes will be losing our land and our livelihoods. Is this the way that progress is intended to work? It seems to be one rule for the rich white people and another for the poor tribes' people!"

The dam builders had expected this stinging but justifiable criticism and were sympathetic to the views now being espoused by the chieftain. It then became clear that they were in fact, fair and reasonable people and had come with a package of genuine offers in order to atone for their loss of land. The spokesman for the dam builders said,

"I agree entirely with your sentiments and it is far from right. Unfortunately, we cannot stop the dam but we can demonstrate our goodwill in helping all of the tribes in a number of ways. We cannot help you physically move but we can show you where you may wish to move to. More importantly, our company will build you a new school and a freshwater pump in the area. Finally, we will provide the funding for an annual scholarship to the high school in the nearest township, to be awarded to every top boy and girl of the senior year, for each village, as long as the dam remains in operation."

The chieftain expressed his gratitude and acknowledged the compensation being pledged – fresh running water!

The dam builders left explaining that they had put white stakes in the ground to show the safer ground to the west. They gave No Hat a blueprint of the dam and its details, as none of the adults could either read or write. Whenever they needed to record anything, like their nation's history and events, such as droughts, famines and tribal battles, they always recorded it in song.

The loss of their land and the coming of the waters would thus be verbally recorded, remembered, revered, regularly chanted and handed down from one generation to the next. The move would mean shifting *everything* at least forty kilometres west – this was no small task.

What about the thousands of animals, who were completely unaware of the traumatic events that awaited them? Had anyone thought of what would happen to them – probably not! It soon became apparent that *no* consideration had been given to the residing animal kingdom. It would be a case of survival of the fittest.

The immediate need was to relocate families and livestock to safer ground. No Hat's father looked in despair at his small plot of land, which had fed them over many years. The school was closed with immediate effect.

'It wasn't *all* bad,' thought No Hat! The reality was that they would be forced to leave *everything they knew*, and move to a strange and distant new land. This of course would include the vast numbers of the largest-living-land-animals-on-the-planet, including Keep Trying! The sheer size of the task just didn't bear thinking about, and was it actually possible?

Eventually and very reluctantly, the village folks and tribal elders began to accept the news and plan for their inevitable move. The dam builders had explained that the dam was now nearing completion.

Soon the river to the south of them would be stemmed, and the natural course of the river would be changed forever. The water would then find its own level and begin to enter and fill their vast plain; the plain that had been their home for countless generations.

For the tribesmen of the valley it was impossible to visualize the dry baked earth beneath their feet, becoming a vast lake.

—∞—

Chapter Two
The reunion

By now the chieftain and the elders had reluctantly accepted the dam builder's advice to move out of the valley as soon as possible and to find somewhere safe for their tribe to live. No Hat asked to accompany the five selected adults on their quest to identify a new site for their village, and other villages would be doing likewise.

The reconnaissance or 'recce' party set off the following morning. It moved at a steady pace all day and had covered a good forty kilometres before the ground began to rise appreciably. The dam builders had calculated that this area would be safe and above the level of the spreading water and recommended this as a possible location.

By now the recce party had reached the higher ground behind which lay a range of hills stretching for many kilometres. The white stakes were there – as promised! The tribesmen now had to have faith that the dam builders would be true to their words, the same men who had taken both their nation's heritage and homes away.

The recce party had found what they were looking for – their mission was accomplished.

After a cold night under the stars, the recce party set off on the journey home. It was going to be another long day on the move, but they were fit and seasoned runners.

They had been running at a comfortable pace for almost an hour, when they came across a small herd of elephants, the same size as a herd they had seen before.

These silent juggernauts were busily engaged in having their extended brunch and didn't seem to be interested in the file of tribesmen passing nearby.

That is, apart from one small elephant, who looked across and said,

"Could that possibly be No Hat?" By this time, the tribesmen had come to a cautionary halt. No Hat looked across at the herd and at one elephant in particular, and thought,

"It couldn't possibly be, but it was – it was Keep Trying!" Simultaneously, they both moved towards each other. Keep Trying waved his trunk and No Hat waved his new straw boater in sheer delight at seeing each other again.

There was a familiar looking bird perched on Keep Trying's rear – a yellow-billed oxpecker. No Hat walked right up to Keep Trying and pulled his ear affectionately. The rest of the herd looked on rather bemused, as our two heroes were so obviously happy to see each other again. The rest of the tribesmen stood with their mouths open, looking in amazement at what they saw happening between No Hat and one of the largest-living-land-animals-on-the-planet.

Once their joint excitement had abated, No Hat tried to explain about the dam and what would happen once the water started to fill the valley. Understandably, Keep Trying found the story totally incomprehensible; and he should know, having walked for five full days to reach a rapidly drying water hole.

Patiently and slowly, No Hat explained about the dam being built and its effect on the river and surrounding lands. It was not an easy task as he didn't really understand the full implications himself. Eventually, after much explaining, Keep

Trying understood and he bobbed and bounced his way back to the herd, to relate this unbelievable story to the matriarch. At the same time, No Hat re-joined his group to explain what they had just seen and what our reunited couple wanted to do.

Nearby, the matriarch went into a huddle with a few long-trusted friends to consider how to execute the 'grand master plan' that had just been hatched by Keep Trying and his newly found long lost friend, No Hat. After a lengthy discussion, Keep Trying and No Hat reconvened, by which time the proposed scheme was agreed. The rest of the recce party stood looking at a baby elephant and a boy who had been deep in conversation together.

The matriarch took a wise but pragmatic approach. After listening to Keep Trying and his story, she agreed that the herd would help the villagers move west. The surrounding grassland and semi-desert would provide lush and plentiful grass, berries and leaves. These rich pickings would keep them satisfied for the next few weeks, before they needed to move on.

Therefore the herd could act as heavyweight porters for the time being at least. The matriarch insisted that there was an agreed understanding between animal and man

– they had different needs! Keep Trying and No Hat were not only thrilled at meeting up again, but it now appeared that they had found a way of helping the villagers move home.

They promised to meet up again, with the oxpecker, at the village when the herd arrived there. After *four years* they had bumped into each other again – it was a chance in a million. The tribesmen set off back towards the village. The herd resumed their foraging for food and amongst them was one very happy young elephant.

The men were still in a state of shock, having seen an elephant and a young boy conversing with each other on quite a difficult subject. They still had nearly a full day ahead of them, with a lot to think about and discuss, like talking elephants, instead of their normal singing and chanting.

The African sun, a perfectly shaped orange ball, was disappearing behind the dark horizon as the recce party arrived home, with such a tale to tell!

—∞—

That night, back in the village, the chieftain called the villagers together, where No Hat described the bewildering events of the day. By now No Hat had become something of a celebrity and when his name was mentioned on a number of occasions, the elders looked and nodded in his direction.

The thought of having to move from the land they and their forefathers had occupied for hundreds of years still hurt and angered them. But fortuitously, the freak meeting of No Hat and Keep Trying had offered them a 'one in a million' opportunity to move to safer higher ground.

These grey gentle giants (*who could also be extremely dangerous – and not gentle at all*) had agreed to be transporters. The dismantled huts and equipment would have been difficult to haul across forty kilometres of rough terrain. For the herd, they would hardly be aware of their cargo. The reunion of No Hat and Keep Trying could bring happiness to many.

Meanwhile, Keep Trying and his mother spent most of the time deep in conversation with the matriarch, who had encountered and overcome many difficult situations in her long lifetime. But this was a new one even for the grand old lady. She instinctively knew that by helping the villagers they might one day help them in return (perhaps by finding ways of getting rid of the terrible ivory poachers). What was that saying 'one good turn deserves another?'

They could also see how much pleasure Keep Trying had got from meeting his long last friend again – so let them make the most of it! Not only was it a joyful reunion for No Hat and Keep Trying, it was the start of their new challenges.

That night No Hat lay on his blanket with his hands folded behind his neck, staring at the roof of his hut. His thoughts kept returning to the magical reunion that he had experienced only a few hours ago. Never in his wildest dreams did he ever *really* believe that he would see Keep Trying again.

Yet, in his heart of hearts, he always hoped that he *might!* He smiled to himself as he thought about what had happened in the last forty-eight hours, and the next adventure that awaited them. He felt no tiredness whatsoever after the long day's run, with any exhaustion replaced by the exhilaration of having been reunited with Keep Trying; sleep would not come easy.

Chapter Three
Heavy helpers

The following morning, No Hat told the other young members of the tribe of the special bond he had established with an *elephant* called Keep Trying. This had happened at a previous marvellous meeting, some four years ago.

He went on to explain that he had asked for the herd's help in moving their village – 'lock, stock and barrel' – to their new home. (No Hat knew that this phrase meant something to do with dismantling rifles, but his only close sighting of a rifle had been of an ivory poacher standing in the bottom of a pit in their first adventure together). They didn't appreciate what he was trying to explain, but had no reason to doubt him, so they thought, 'Let's wait and see.'

Many of the villagers remained deeply sceptical and wary as they had vivid memories of how dangerous and destructive elephants could be. The older members were difficult to convince – more so than the elephants!

All too often, bones had been broken and barriers had been battered by these hulking, powerful and at times uncaring beasts. Some of the older members still remembered when a small herd trampled its way across a corner of the village, completely destroying huts and leaving a scene of disaster in their wake.

In the following days there was a marked difference in the level of activity taking place in the two camps. For the elephants, life went on in exactly the same way, with everyone continually eating, whilst the herd made slow but steady progress towards the village. Keep Trying's moment of glory had been short-lived, even if his mother was both surprised by, and proud of, him. Now he had resumed his position as a junior member of the herd, with just a bit of envy from the other young elephants. The matriarch calmly turned the herd east, in gentle increments of direction, so as not to make it too obvious that the water hole was no longer their destination.

She did not act deviously, as they all knew her too well and they trusted her with their lives. On many occasions, they had been forced to follow her for weeks on end without food or water. Their trust in her was total and implicit and she had never let them down.

Somewhere in the dark recesses of her ageing mind she had stored and retained the exact location of that valuable of most commodities – water. The convoy of elephants headed towards the villagers, with time to forage - soon they would have other things to do!   Keep Trying was absolutely thrilled to have recognised No Hat and their chance reunion. He repeated to himself,

"It is four years since we had said goodbye to each other."

The chieftain of the village was not the head of his community by accident. He was most certainly the oldest and most venerated leader, highly respected and held in great esteem by all surrounding villagers.   He had been the chieftain for more years than he could remember. He was now an old man.

Once a tall and powerful figure, his frail body had shrunk in size and was now almost skeletal, with his skin wrapped around his painfully thin frame like some valuable parchment, a sure tell-tale sign of age. On one thigh he carried a large and ugly scar, and on one shoulder the outline and indentations of teeth marks were still clear to see, after so many years. They were both the results of hunting forays that had gone awry.

He would never elaborate, accepting that hunting was part of their way of life and the outcome was not always one-sided, with finely balanced dangers and gains. Like all hunters he respected *all* animals – big and small, and understood the law of the grasslands, where each creature had its own life to live, and the instinct to survive.

He was almost bald, his head a shining polished surface of dark mahogany, save for a few remaining wisps of grey hair. His grin revealed one solitary tooth that had been virtually eaten away by time and decay. Yet his eyes were sparklingly clear and his thoughts lucid. Whilst his body may have diminished with age, his brain certainly had not.

He had out-lived his dear wife by many seasons, but he still lived in the same hut, in the same village, where he had spent his entire life. His son (and eventual successor) and his grandchildren, did a good job of looking after him, catering for his every need in a loving and caring way without it being a chore or a duty.

Now in the privacy of his hut he worried about what had to be done, what lay ahead for his tribe, and whether he was doing the right thing by them He knew his judgement and decision on the move was a major milestone in the history of his people. He had no fear for himself - he knew that his hut would soon enough become empty. He just wanted to do the *right* thing for his village, as he had always tried to do.

What he did bring to the villagers was calm reassurance, advising them about what had to be done rather than telling them what to do. They trusted his wisdom and listened to his advice. The chieftain was aware that it takes a lot longer to create and build a village than it does to dismantle it, no — to destroy a village! But if moving was the right thing to do, then that is what they would do, with the assistance of some heavy helpers.

—∞—

The villagers divided themselves into groups with relations, family friends and friends naturally gravitating towards each other. An irate neighbour from another village arrived questioning the very *need* for the move and the upheaval it would cause.

He had visited the nearest point of the river, to see if there was indeed any truth in what the dam builders had said. He saw no changes in the river whatsoever; perhaps it was all some clever and devious ploy, he thought, just to get the villagers to move from their land, so that they could use it for other things. He had an authoritative voice and he spoke with such conviction that he had persuaded his village to remain where they were, and suggested that No Hat's village may wish to reconsider.

The chieftain, however, was in no doubt; indeed he had known the dam was being built for many months. He had not wanted to mention it to the elders, for fear of causing panic, not until he was sure and knew how far the waters would reach. It had been a closely guarded and difficult secret.

He was not going to be detracted or influenced by a notorious 'hot-head', who was known for causing unnecessary friction within his own village. The problem was that his arguments and reasoning were plausible, and this gave rise to more doubt and unrest in those who just wanted to be reassured.

The village hunting parties had already reported seeing a massive concrete construction across the neck of the gorge. His worst fears were now confirmed and they must not delay a *moment* longer. Two families moved into one hut, and the villagers carefully took the other apart, strut by strut, piece by piece, frond by frond.

Eventually, all the dismantled sections were then bound and tied into sizeable but manageable bundles, which would sit comfortably on either side of an elephant's back.

The chieftain had one terrible thought,

'What happens now if the elephants don't come!'

Improvised cages and boxes were made for the livestock. The goats and dogs needed little help or persuasion; they could stand on their own four feet. The chickens were far more reluctant and needed more than a gentle coaxing to enter their ad hoc travelling arrangements — an odd assortment of wooden boxes and wired cages. Many of the older villagers found it difficult to accept that a herd of elephants was going to help to move them.

—∞—

Chapter Four
Up sticks

After a few days, all that was left was the perimeter fencing which comprised tall stout poles, and the empty and dilapidated huts belonging to their ancestors and which were still occupied by their spirits. They would surely turn in their graves at the scene being played out before them. It was a sad and pitiful sight to behold.

No Hat's father had salvaged all that he could from his parched plot of land; he now had the prospect of having to start all over again. All that now remained were a few crops which were not deemed worthy of saving. He stared at the ground, reminded of what it had both given and taken – it was a sad day indeed. He then lifted his head, held his shoulders back and walked away - without so much as a single backwards glance!

As if on cue, the herd appeared in the distance; the matriarch had been as good as her word, but had anyone really ever doubted her? No Hat was again elevated in stature, and sent forward to greet the huge grey delegation and work force. Keep Trying had likewise been despatched ahead of the herd. Without hesitation or invitation Keep

Trying lifted a foreleg and No Hat jumped nimbly onboard and assumed his customary position on Keep Trying's back. This friendly display went someway to assuaging the doubts, and soothing the fears and concerns of the wary and cautious villagers. Most stood flabbergasted at the sight of Keep Trying and No Hat becoming a single entity!

The herd then made its sedate and unhurried progress to the edge of what was left of the village, to see what still had to be done. All that remained were the sturdy fence poles that acted as a partial deterrent and protective barrier against any invading animals such as the largest-living-land-animals-on-the-planet: elephants!

Once the poles had gone, all that would remain would be the fragile and forlorn huts belonging to their long-departed ancestors, whose spirits were still living there. These beloved and broken monuments would surely just float away when the waters arrived. Their nearby graves would soon be covered by the lake – this would be the closest most of them had ever got to water!

—∞—

The bare and worn patches of ground showed where many cup finals had been played – there would be no more 'extra time and penalty shoot outs' from here! The villagers stood around in groups, still wary, visibly agitated, unconvinced and anxious about their move. Up until this moment they had always treated these great, lumbering beasts with fear and trepidation. But now their trusted chieftain was telling them that their erstwhile enemies were going to *help* them move to their new homes.

In a matter of days their world had completely turned upside down. Why did those dam builders have to come in the first place? For the younger members it presented a new challenge, but for the ageing populace it was the worst possible thing to have inflicted upon them – they felt too old and tired to start again.

It was, therefore, a rather gloomy and despondent group of villagers that the herd met when they arrived, although the lukewarm reception didn't seem to bother them unduly. These tribal people wondered exactly what lay in store for them. Their futures were very much in the lap of the gods – who seemed for the time being to have deserted them! The chieftain and elders had already explained to No Hat what help they needed, and had asked him, with the aid of his friend, Keep Trying, to act as the go-between for the two groups. No Hat understood immediately what was required of him and his 'partner in crime' and went off to confer with Keep Trying, who then briefed the matriarch.

The matriarch didn't need to be told, she had already started to walk around the herd, outlining the 'plan of action'. The first task was to dismantle the poled stockade; these wooden sentinels would be needed at the next village. The closely fixed stanchions had been in the ground for many years, and were far too heavy and robust to be moved by the villagers.

Three of the larger elephants leaned against the fence, and then with enormous strength, pulled the weathered timbers clean out of the ground with their mighty trunks. It was the most awesome display of raw power!

Within the space of thirty minutes, the fence resembled a pile of matchsticks, strewn haphazardly across the ground. This was indeed the end of the village which had been the only home for many of the villagers. The elephants didn't understand what all the fuss was about.

Keep Trying, with his best friend No Hat onboard, then walked around the outside of the herd, nudging the elephants nearer to the waiting cargoes. They acted like a sheep dog rounding up a flock of sheep, but these were no *woolly jumpers!!*

This was the first close contact the tribesmen and the herd had had with each other. The elephants were very generous, and stood calmly by, as the remnants of the village were loaded onto their backs.

The task of carrying the heavy poles fell to the larger elephants. The villagers watched from a distance as their dismantled homes were secured by a few tribesmen, who had gained enough confidence to work close up to the elephants.

No Hat and Keep Trying, in their role of 'mounted supervisors', moved from one elephant to another overseeing the loading. The weight was no problem whatsoever, the important thing was not to upset or frighten these large grey transporters – they had never before been approached, let alone touched!

—∞—

The same could be said of the tribesmen, who grew in confidence, only when Keep Trying and No Hat were close to them. Even the very heavy poles were successfully mounted and secured onto the strongest of the heavyweight leviathans. The villagers had taken the sensible precaution of keeping the other animals well apart from each other.

The last thing anyone wanted was for any of the cows, oxen or goats to come into accidental contact with the heavy helpers. The chickens, however, remained a law unto themselves, and continued to wander everywhere, and into everyone, completely fearless of their size.

But throughout this frenetic period of activity it was quite clear to both animal and man, that our two heroes No Hat and Keep Trying held some unique bond of understanding between them, and it was working. Without this partnership, the whole venture could never have even been entertained, let alone got off the ground!

No Hat's friends and other youngsters thought it was all some huge adventure. They did, however, see what a major role No Hat and Keep Trying were playing in their supervisory role and were determined to play their own worthwhile part; No Hat and Keep Trying shouldn't be allowed to steal all of the limelight.

To this end they kindly offered their willing services to the older and less able members of the tribe. Many of the older villagers still found it difficult to accept what had happened to their simple lives, all in a matter of days. They stopped agog and marvelled when they saw an elephant and a boy talking to each other.

First they were told that their dry dust bowl of a valley would become a vast lake. Then they were being told that when they get to their new village, wherever that may be, there would be a constant supply of fresh water and a brand new school. Whilst not forgetting to mention that a *herd of elephants* would be transporting their huts and belongings some forty kilometres westward. The world was going crazy!

Chapter Five
The exodus

By the time the sun was high in the sky, it was time for the herd of the largest-living-land-animals-on-the-planet to head west. They would be accompanied at a distance by the eighty or so villagers of all ages. The speed of the convoy was that of the slowest mover.

The expected journey time to cover the forty or so kilometres was approximately three full days, with hopefully only two overnight stops. All of the adult elephants, except one (being matriarch had *some* privileges) were now fully loaded with the cargo of disbanded huts, whilst the younger elephants only had themselves to carry.

The matriarch led the herd away. The villagers paused until there was a gap of about two hundred metres between them and the herd of elephants, so as to avoid any unnecessary misunderstandings. Then they set off, most of them with large bundles balanced effortlessly on their heads. The villages' other larger animals made their way in a tethered line behind them.

The caravan, consisting of two separate but unified groups, was on its way.

At the end of the first two days walk, the pattern of activity was repeated. Each family established a make-shift camp, collecting wood, lighting fires, cooking and eating hot mealie – their staple diet made from finely ground maize.

The tired and weary travellers then tried to sleep, either under trees or huddled in blankets beside roaring fires. The smell of burning wood was strong in the air, with smoke drifting away into the night. The fires both kept away any would-be attackers and helped to keep out the bitter cold of the African nights – but not completely!

The elephants did not have a problem with the cold. The older folks cheered up appreciably once they were on the move. They set a fine example to the youngsters, coping stoically with the daily twenty kilometres or so walk, and the improvised sleeping arrangements. The youngsters were a credit to their parents, helping wherever and whenever they could. With the chieftain's words of encouragement, the two caravans continued to move west.

The elephants were unaffected by the extra responsibility and weight of luggage they had been given. At night they just wandered a little way off to while away the time quietly and to eat. No Hat and Keep Trying met up for friendly progress reports and then spent some time together – as good friends do! Despite the warmth and comfort of many layers of blankets, the cold African nights still found a way of chilling everyone to the bone.

Not surprisingly, getting the human convoy underway in the morning was not a problem. Everyone was eager to get moving. Breakfast was not a luxury they could afford to spend time on. Great minds think alike, and No Hat and Keep Trying met going towards each other. Without further ado, No Hat was onboard, by which time the matriarch had begun to move off to the west.

How did she *know* what direction they were heading - had Keep Trying told her? Keep Trying with No Hat *and* a reappearing oxpecker on his back spent the day moving between the two groups. Their encouragement and enthusiasm was a welcome fillip to the tribes' people, particularly the older members, but the herd remained unaffected. For the second day the strange caravan of elephants and tribesmen continued to make good progress.

On the morning of the third day, the chieftain made a surprising request to No Hat,

"Can I sit behind you on Keep Trying's back?" The oldest and most senior member of the tribe was prepared to follow the example of one of his youngsters. No

Hat helped the chieftain onboard. He was only a small additional weight, but he was a very valuable passenger.

The rest of the human express watched in wonder as Keep Trying then set off at a brisk pace, complete with his *two* passengers. The oxpecker hurriedly departed deciding that, 'Two's company - three's a crowd!'

There was of course, method in the chieftain's madness: he wanted to get ahead of everyone and decide, without fear or favour, upon the most suitable site for their next village. Within a matter of minutes he relaxed his grip around No Hat's waist and sat balanced, reasonably comfortable and unaided.

Later, some considerable distance on, he noticed that the ground rose slightly towards the bottom edge of a range of hills that ran the entire length of the gorge. He saw the white marker posts and knew he had found precisely what he was looking for.

He decided on his village's next location, as was his duty as the tribal chieftain. In this way, there would be no squabbling amongst the few hot heads in his village, As he climbed down from Keep Trying he graciously thanked him for this 'once in a lifetime' experience, but he was inwardly glad that he didn't have to do it all again!

Sometime later the two groups arrived: the elephants with their valuable cargoes, looking none the worse for their ladened journey, followed by the weary tribe. Some of the older villagers were showing signs of fatigue after being on the go for three days.

The livestock was just happy to have arrived and to have some freedom to roam and explore their new surroundings. The villagers were impressed and approved of their chieftain's choice of location.

Keep Trying raised his trunk and waved it in delight, as if to say, 'That is a job well done!'

Later, when the heat of the day had gone, they set up camp and once more lit fires. In the morning they would start the exciting task of building their new homes and begin their future. In the meantime, the herd remained quite unaffected by their loads. Again they wandered off to start their supper. No Hat dismounted from his faithful friend Keep Trying; the elephant then joined his herd and the young lad returned to his mother and their camp.

It was a surreal situation, yet everyone seemed to know and accept what had to be done. The matriarch was pleased by the way in which her herd had adapted to their roles in the exodus. As the families made the best of their sleeping arrangements, the chieftain wandered from one camp fire to another.

He was exhausted, but it was something he needed to do. He felt genuine care and concern for his extended family – although in all truth he needed care himself. He thanked them all for their support and congratulated them on the admirable way they had coped with the three days on the road. Tomorrow would be the first day in their new village!

—∞—

Chapter Six
The chieftain's hut

The following day, the new site really did look as if a circus had arrived in town! It was a noisy and hectic scene of activity. Keep Trying and No Hat oversaw the unloading and positioning of the cargoes that would soon grow into their huts.

The elephants, under the ever-watchful eye of the matriarch, enjoyed pounding the poles into the ground, presumably to keep animals exactly like themselves out. Remarkably, by mid-afternoon the area already resembled a village.

The position of each hut had been pegged out, and the chickens had staked out their new territory. The young lads had even decided where the next football pitch would be situated; unless of course - *the grown-ups decided to move the goal posts!!*

In keeping with tribal custom, the first hut to be built was that of the chieftain's. In this particular case it was also borne out of need and necessity. The chieftain now sat at the base of a tree totally exhausted and physically spent. A couple of tribe's women wrapped him in a blanket and encouraged him to take a little sustenance. The super-human effort required from him to mount and ride Keep Trying, and the manner in which he had remained onboard, had clearly taken its toll. It had drained every last drop of energy from him.

No Hat thought it was the culmination of both the physical demands and the mental worry - the boy had an old head on his young shoulders. The chieftain asked for his hut could be built in a quiet secluded corner of what would eventually be the village compound. In keeping with his style of leadership, he preferred to be unobtrusive and unassuming - keeping himself to himself.

He had always remembered what his father had told him: 'Good leadership is the art of getting things done through willing cooperation, not by force or coercion.' He had heeded these wise words and always led by asking, not telling. This style of management had served him well over many years, where he had adopted a low-profile and non-interfering role. There had been few occasions when he had been called upon to arbitrate over some petty squabble; proof indeed of a good leader, if at all proof was needed.

Building his hut was a sight to behold. All the able-bodied men set to with gusto and within two hours the first hut of the new village stood proudly erect.

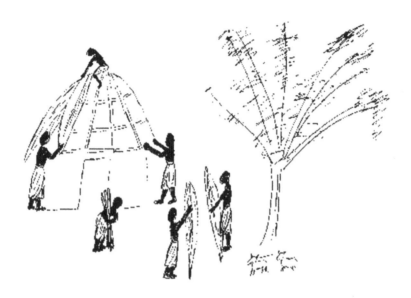

They gently carried the chieftain into his new home to the resounding cheers of his tribe, and carefully lowered him onto his favourite blanket. The old man was overcome with gratitude and shooed everyone out, urging them to get on with the task of building their own huts. In the meantime, the grandchildren and women lovingly made their chieftain a log fire and a small helping of mealie.

Now lying comfortably in his new home he reviewed the recent events and what they had achieved since the initial shock and the sudden upheaval of his entire community. He was extremely pleased by the way in which the move had gone; they were here without any injuries or violent dissenters.

This was not the case in at least one village, where the whole rationale of 'up sticks' had been vehemently questioned and the entire village had refused to budge. It had only taken a few vitriolic words from a doubting and dissenting few, questioning the very wisdom of such a move, to persuade the many!

Alone on his blanket, the chieftain candidly admitted to a complete lack of confidence in No Hat and Keep Trying's proposal. It was a proposal made on the spur of the moment, when their adrenalin was high and they were excited at being reunited. Nevertheless, he recognized that the offer was made with enthusiasm, good faith and the best of intentions, and there were no better suggestions on the table. However, based on his many years of knowledge and experiences of brushes and near-misses with the largest-living-land-animals-on-the-planet – he thought that the idea of moving an entire village using elephants was not a practical possibility.

In the event, he and the elders went along with the plan out of sheer desperation. No one had *seriously* thought of using elephants, the very idea was just too preposterous! But the chieftain and elders had been proven wrong. Here they were — his extended family: a hundred tribal men, women, children and livestock, all safely installed in their new village and safe from the spreading waters.

Moreover, they were now erecting their same huts, which had survived being dismantled and transported on the backs of elephants! It was a plan fraught with problems and danger, yet it had succeeded. It had also demonstrated the resilience and fortitude of his tribe in coping so well in the face of such adversity. The chieftain suddenly sat bolt upright and smacked his forehead theatrically with the open palm of his wrinkled hand. He had just realized how such an audacious undertaking was possible — it was as plain as the nose on his face — his ancestors, had after all, made the journey with them!

His silent prayers had been answered! Thank goodness for the guardianship of their great tribal spirits and the exuberance and daring of youth. He could now stop worrying; otherwise it would be the death of him. He smiled at his own wisdom, at having answered his own questions. Lying down, the chieftain contentedly fell asleep.

Chapter Seven
Getting back to normal

The village was just one of the many that were now emerging every five kilometres or so along the edge of the protecting hills. The water was a safe kilometre away, on a much lower level. The dam builders had been as good as their word, and had visited the tribe's people to confirm and assure them that their new but growing conurbations were safe from the relentless spread of water.

Now with all these new villages springing up,

'I suppose it won't be too long before they start work on the pumping station and the new school building,' thought No Hat with mixed emotions! Inwardly he admitted that lessons were now really enjoyable, with each day at school giving him increased knowledge. But for the time being he just wanted to spend every possible moment that he could with Keep Trying.

Within a matter of days the village looked as if it had always been there. Each hut had adjoining pens for their most treasured possessions; their livestock. The goats and chickens had long decided that it was best to just ignore each other, and were exploring their new homes. The cows and oxen were now securely corralled in a fenced area, thanks to the efforts of the herd, courtesy of the matriarch, No Hat, Keep Trying and the tribe's people.

Tracks were already becoming defined between villages and life really did look as if it was getting back to normal. The older men and women were now fully recovered from what had been a gruelling three day trek. What would they have done without the help of the elephants – they were now seeing these mighty beasts in another light.

The boys had already played their first game of football with the inevitable number of grazed knees. However, before the first match could kick off they had to remove a number of bushes and small trees. Here again the brute force and talent of many trunks saved many hours of work. It would be fair to say, however, that the pitch needed further groundwork before they could invite any of the other village teams to visit. In the meantime some of Keep Trying's other large grey friends were more than pleased to eat or remove any unwanted bushes or trees. The new football pitch was a great success and soon they had played their first home game of the season. The season lasted for twelve months!

No Hat's father was again a happy man. He had found and secured an area of land that he could work on and turn into a cultivated plot. But before any plants could be planted, there lay ahead many weeks of back-breaking work, clearing and preparing the ground, and any crops would be many months away.

No Hat offered to help, but not with any real enthusiasm, and almost looked forward to going back to school, because of the amount of hard work still to be done in clearing the land. Keep Trying certainly helped and removed all of the unwanted bushes in no time at all. He then dragged them away to a quiet spot to eat them.

Keep Trying wittily remarked,

"Waste not want not!" (It was No Hat's father's favourite expression and one he had heard him use on more than one occasion). No Hat, not to be outdone by his four-legged companion, helped by collecting a plentiful supply of elephant dung and making a huge compost heap for his father's future use.

The elephants had now become used to the nearness of the tribesmen, as long as they both kept a respectable distance apart from each other - mindful not to take this

131

new status quo for granted. They worked and coexisted with relative ease, largely due to the carefree comings and goings of No Hat and Keep Trying.

Our two heroes were asked to supervise the herd's work which they willingly did. It still left them time to share together, for they both knew the herd would soon move on. The perimeter fence was now almost complete; the larger elephants had done a superb job of pounding in the many dozens of posts, being careful not to box themselves in.

Many of the tribesmen stood watching as the elephants demonstrated the awesome power and flexibility of their trunks. Whilst out-and-about onboard Keep Trying, No Hat looked at his village people and realised that there were no male elephants in the herd, except of course Keep Trying and a couple of other younger males,

"Why is that," he asked? Keep Trying explained in a very matter-of-fact way,

"One day my father started to drift away onto the edge of the herd. He would disappear for days, sometimes for weeks on end, and then finally he disappeared completely, to begin a largely solitary existence. He will be living alone like most of the other male elephants. I suppose it will happen to me one day," he added, rather sadly. "This has left me with my mother in virtually a completely female environment. Eventually, even my sister and the older female calves will break away from the herd and form their own smaller groups. But *I'm* going to be my mother's boy for a number of years to come!"

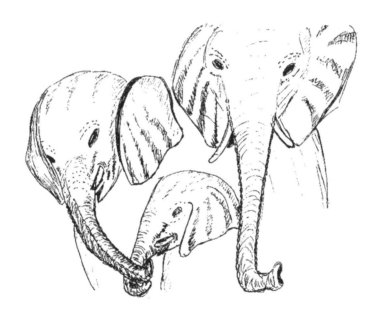

No Hat listened in silence, trying to understand the mind and workings of these majestic animals. How had these intelligent largest-living-land-animals-on-the-planet evolved over thousands of years and survived; for the most part in a largely separate and isolated society?

No Hat then turned to Keep Trying and said in a conspiratorial tone,

"*Now* let me tell you something about, *you know who,*" as he pointed his finger back over his shoulder!

"At school today we learnt all about our favourite friend – yes, the oxpecker." With that they both turned to check whether their faithful feathered companion was still there and he was.

"We were told," said No Hat, "By one of our best teachers that these very chatty birds usually reside on giraffes, buffalos, rhinos, or on the backs of other large mammals, but *not* on elephants. In fact elephants will actively dislodge the oxpecker when it tries to land, so how come, Keep Trying, our oxpecker doesn't bother you one iota? In all our time together I have *never* seen you once object."

Keep Trying was quite ambivalent, "I suppose he can be irksome (*where did he learn such words*) at times, but I've come to accept him as part of our team. He certainly doesn't do me any harm and actually he does me a favour and gets rid of my unwanted parasites, and I don't mean *you* No Hat!" They both laughed at Keep Trying's joke.

No Hat shook his head, impressed by his friend's humour and intelligence and thought to himself, 'He really *is* the most remarkable elephant.'

It did seem as if the oxpecker knew that he was being talked about, and it did look to be the very same bird. He had a short thick yellow bill - probably the reason why he was called a yellow-billed oxpecker! At the end of his beak there was a distinctive red tip, with matching bright red eyes and clearly defined yellow circles of flesh around them. No Hat continued,

"The teacher also told us that oxpeckers collect hair from their host to line their tree nests, or else they dwell in readily accessible rock-holes." To emphasize the point and show how much he had paid attention, he said they laid between three and five white to pale brown-spotted eggs per clutch. No Hat explained that the oxpecker is highly adapted to life on its host and even does its courting whilst it is on its carrier. Thankfully, up until now No Hat and Keep Trying had been spared the complication of a feathered romance!

"Also, it was not uncommon to see three or four oxpeckers on an animal's back at any one time, so we must be grateful for small mercies" said No Hat.

They both laughed out loud, happy to be sharing each other's company – the three of them! In the meantime, the non-laughing member of the team (his ears still burning) continued to peck away at the many ticks and larvae residing in Keep Trying's back, unaware that he was the butt of his two friends amusement.

Chapter Eight
Spreading water

With the village complete and the herd still content to graze in the vicinity, No Hat and Keep Trying had the time and the opportunity to explore. Both Keep Trying's and No Hat's mothers were happy with this arrangement.

Indeed the herd and village were now well accustomed to seeing our inseparable duo, as they appeared to be, here there and everywhere, as too were the many oxpeckers. No Hat and Keep Trying's fame had travelled down the entire valley, and the other villagers were no longer surprised to see an elephant and young boy enjoying each other's company. There was little envy or jealously from the other boys. They were quite happy just to keep their distance and marvel at the unusual friendship.

No Hat and Keep Trying had now come to accept and indeed *expect* the company of their constant companion: the oxpecker. On the occasions when he flew off he always landed back at the first sign of any movement. He seemed to have a flight plan for every possible contingency. No Hat always remembered their first adventure and the role that their little feathered-friend had played; in particular, when he had spotted the herd when Keep Trying was lost.

Now there were a number of oxpeckers accompanying the herd, (despite the elephants' objections) but the same one had decided to stay with Keep Trying and No Hat. They both thought it was the same oxpecker, they could never be sure, but it looked and acted like him – and he was always welcome!

It was during one of their outings that No Hat learnt that school would be resuming in a few days' time. They had no school room but lessons would be held under a large spreading tree which offered a fair measure of shade. One of the dam builders had visited the chieftain with mixed news. He was pleased to report that work on the school building would start in the next few months, but the pumping station was still a long way off. Unfortunately, it had been low down on the dam builders list of priorities. He also informed the villagers that the dam was now complete and working. Yes, their old village *was* now underwater, but it would take the next five years to fill the valley completely. He also admitted that little prior consideration had been given to saving the many thousands of animals that had now moved to islands of higher ground!

On the way back from one of their many excursions, Keep Trying took it upon himself to head slightly uphill and into new territory. They had not been walking long when they saw something glitter, like the sun reflecting on a mirror, and they heard the gentle sound of running water.

They had stumbled upon a small spring, rising in the base of the foothills and meandering downwards into what could barely be described as a stream. The cool, fresh, clean running water was a marvellous discovery, and without doubt it would become the headquarters for all future village meetings.

Keep Trying and No Hat would be the toast of all the villages, once they all knew. They couldn't wait to get back to the village, to tell everyone of this stupendous discovery.

But first the two of them had paused to enjoy their first refreshing drink, and a bath for the third member, the ever-present oxpecker, from this their *own* spring. Keep Trying had never moved so fast, although it was not exactly as fast as in a stampede! Hurrying back to No Hat's new village, whilst still trying to contain their excitement at their discovery, they came across a large procession of tribesmen, heavily ladened down with their belongings: what was going on?

Approaching them was *the* vociferous loud-mouth whom No Hat's chieftain had met some weeks earlier; he had ridiculed the whole idea of the gorge being filled with water. He had openly mocked the claim being made by the dam builders and had persuaded his village folk not to move, believing it to be some trick. He was now a humble person as he explained what had happened and the scene he had witnessed with his own eyes. His disgruntled villagers listened to their apologetic leader, knowing they had been wrong to have been persuaded by him to remain in their villages and not move.

Only a few days earlier, he and his hunting party had ventured south and seen a shimmering light in the far distance. It looked like the reflection of sunlight on glass: it was water! As they got nearer they could clearly see that the water was creeping inexorably across the lower ground which was baked dry by the sun, soon to be the start of new river beds.

It appeared to be slow, relentless and unending, as the leading edge moved further and wider. It was only moving a few metres at the most, but obviously increasing in depth all the time. Already animals were moving from the lower to the higher ground, and islands were beginning to appear.

His was the only village not to have heeded the advice and now they were forced to make their way west with a degree of urgency.

"Already," he told them, "The water was approaching what had been *their* village." The dam builders had been right after all! The Doubting Thomas left with his far from happy villagers.

They *knew* they would now have difficulty in finding a suitable new village site, as all the prime positions had already been taken. No Hat noticed that the dejected villagers only had with them what personal belongings they could carry. Their huts had been left and abandoned, awaiting the sure destiny of being submerged by the ever-increasing lake. They would have to rebuild from scratch, with what they could find; as the preceding villagers would have surely scoured the surrounding area for any available building materials. How lucky No Hat and his village were to have had the help of Keep Trying and his herd!

On No Hat and Keep Trying's return, the chieftain and the villagers received the news of the spreading water. The villagers were thankful for their chieftain's foresight and wisdom to re-locate at precisely the right time; with of course the tremendous help of Keep Trying and his herd. They were also delighted to learn of the fresh running stream nearby.

The chieftain remarked,

"When eventually the dam builders install the pumping station we, and the other villages, will be spoilt for choice. In the meantime we have Keep Trying to thank for discovering our own supply of the nectar of life – water!"

—∞—

The sun had appeared every day for the past four billion years or more, and it followed that it would continue to do so. The matriarch informed her herd that their work was done, their detour had been much appreciated and now they deserved a well-earned mud bath. At the same time she indicated that with the rising of the sun for the third time from now, as it surely must, it would be prudent and timely for the herd to move on. Reluctantly, No Hat and Keep Trying were resigned to the fact that a farewell was indeed imminent.

The matriarch was becoming increasingly aware that the herd was getting restless and in need of somewhere else to eat and bathe. However, before the luxury of a visit to a water hole was possible, there was a small matter of two long weeks of walking, with little or no time for food or water.

Thank goodness Keep Trying was now on full milk rations from his mother! It would also entail an undeclared detour to visit some ancestral bones of their forefathers – *but only the matriarch was aware of this intention.*

She had not let on that she had not been feeling well for some time, and had put it down to her old age. It was time to move on and away from the threat of the spreading water. They would leave in three days' time.

—∞—

Chapter Nine
Pause for thought

With a known deadline, and the inevitable floods of tears that would surely dampen their cheeks when they had to say goodbye, No Hat and Keep Trying were determined to spend every possible moment of the next two days together.

This remaining time would of course have to be shared with the company of their persistent but favourite yellow-billed oxpecker; a feathered friend who had, after all, already proved himself to be a valuable third member of the trio. Perhaps he was booking his ticket for a forthcoming journey?

No Hat and Keep Trying agreed this time they would *not* say goodbye, preferring to think positively, believing one day they *would* meet up again. They both knew the herd's journey to the watering hole was only a staging post stop. The matriarch remembered many distant grazing lands that had yet to be revisited. It could be many months, perhaps years, before the herd turned this way again.

By then they both knew the waters would stretch further into the gorge - wider and deeper. Their fervent hope was that the herd *would* eventually retrace its steps along the edge of the villages. No Hat intimated to Keep Trying that any likelihood of this happening depended on his constant reminders to his mother and, more importantly, the matriarch. Keep Trying retorted saying,

"He knew exactly what had to be said and done," and pointedly reminded No Hat, "We elephants never forget!" In the end, they both agreed to make every effort to make a third meeting, not a chance in a million, but a realistic aspiration, as decreed by one of the largest-living-land-animals-on-the-planet.

No Hat and Keep Trying had taken themselves off to the solitude of the lake (where Keep Trying had enjoyed his wallow), knowing that they would not be disturbed. Both had expressed a wish to be alone together, (they accepted the ever-presence of the oxpecker), to afford themselves the opportunity and the space to reflect and confide in each other in a deeply personal manner.

The faithful yellow-billed oxpecker was the only living person to hear the fascinating and intimate dialogue that ensued between our two heroes. It was a meeting of hearts and minds that went much further than just their many scrapes and adventures together. They opened up to their most inner of thoughts, each revealing how their relationship had changed and improved them as individuals – and made them better people.

Pointing to the water No Hat said,

"This has changed our lives and what's more, we as a tribe owe it to you and your herd for the one chance in a million of making such a fresh start possible. Who would have thought that our chance meeting and idea of using your herd as transporters would have resulted in such a turn of events?" Keep Trying didn't immediately reply then said,

"To be honest I didn't actually think it would work, or that the matriarch would agree to it. Obviously, she was older and wiser and was proved right. But didn't we have some fun doing it!"

Keep Trying stood looking out at the vast expanse of water and asked No Hat,

"Hand on heart, did you *really* think we were going to make it across that river? Because I can tell you now, I had my doubts. When I first slipped into the water I was pleasantly surprised how easy I found it was to swim. But when we started to get pushed sideways towards the waterfall, I really didn't know if I had either the strength or the ability to get to the other side." No Hat replied,

"I'm glad you're telling me now and not then, because I was absolutely petrified." There followed a few minutes of complete silence, as they both re-lived the frightening ordeal, where their trust in each other had again been evident.

No Hat then tried to explain to Keep Trying how his tribe had reacted to the sight of seeing him with an elephant, *talking* to each other. Surely, having considered everything we had done and achieved together, the fact that we can communicate has to be the one outstanding feature of our marvellous relationship. Do you agree, and what does the rest of your herd think about our unique partnership?"

Keep Trying merely smiled. No Hat continued,

"When I got back to the village and told the chieftain and the elders, I could tell they didn't believe a word I was saying. I even began to doubt my own sanity! In fact the only one who was considered creditable was the (he pointed back over his shoulder) oxpecker. But what *has* changed dramatically is the attitude and respect that my villagers now have for you and your herd, as long as they can still keep their distance." They both laughed and the oxpecker looked up to see what all the fuss was about.

For a while they walked back in silence towards the village and the herd: No Hat, Keep Trying and the oxpecker. Then, No Hat quietly uttered the following profound words,

"Memories don't keep you, but no one can take them away." These were the words that their chieftain would often finish a story or statement with, as if to make some special point of significance. The villagers would invariably smile as they had heard it many times.

Keep Trying didn't smile on this occasion, both he and No Hat knew that they *did* indeed have some very special memories, which no one could ever take away from them.

—∞—

Chapter Ten
All's well that ends well

The night before No Hat slept fitfully, conscious of Keep Trying and the herd's impending departure in a few hours' time. His parents could hear him tossing and turning throughout the night and were fully aware of what their son was thinking and going through, but knew that this was one milestone that he had to deal with on his own.

It was, therefore, no surprise to his parents, when No Hat rose and quietly left their hut whilst it was still dark, seeking out Keep Trying who was foraging nearby. In the silent, black and cold African night, the boy and the elephant spent a full hour in private conversation. What they talked about remains their secret. No Hat then returned to his family hut to wait for the herd's inevitable departure, with his parents feigning sleep.

The sun rose on this, the matriarch's third day, as too did No Hat. The herd slowly formed their customary single file, as they shuffled unhurriedly into their familiar and allotted places in the line. No Hat noticed the entire herd was a definite brown in colour. Their true colour was completely camouflaged under a layer of dust and sand, accumulated over many weeks. Without doubt, each of these largest-living-land-animals-on-the-planet was long overdue a visit to the baths, which they had earned – in no small way - as heavy helpers.

The village was beginning to stir and already there were other early risers, mainly comprising of No Hat's peers, who had gathered around to give moral support. Their kind and thoughtful gesture was not lost on No Hat.

For some reason, possibly in a display of farewell recognition and appreciation, the matriarch directed Keep Trying to take his place immediately behind her. This was a nice touch by the sage leader and acknowledged by his mother.

By now, and almost spontaneously, the entire village population had emerged from their huts and assembled either side of the track that led to nowhere. They all stood in silence, watching the departure of these majestic animals as they started to lumber past. The villagers knew exactly how deeply indebted they were to these grey battleships – they no longer thought of them as destroyers!!

Everyone was aware of the significance of the occasion; the continual thuds of elephants' feet hitting the ground added to the drama. The matriarch stopped when Keep Trying was directly in front of No Hat. This enabled our two heroes to say a last - but hopefully not a final - goodbye to each other. The atmosphere was heavily charged, as the entire village stood silent, conscious of the scene being enacted before them, by a *talking elephant* and his best friend – a thirteen-year old boy!

No Hat tugged one of Keep Trying's ears affectionately *(ears that had grown considerably in size over the past four years)* and said,

"Remember what we promised each other this morning and when we crossed the river, you said, 'hang on I won't let you down,' well I won't let you down either. I'll be watching and waiting for your return – whenever that may be. Good luck my dear friend - until we meet again."

Just then the chieftain arrived alongside No Hat. It was the first time for many weeks that the village leader had been seen outside of his hut. The chieftain paused to get his breath back and recover his composure, leaning heavily on a walking stick. The prop was his hunting spear, which had been cut down and reshaped to fit his now diminutive size. The villagers knew just how much effort it had taken for the chieftain to make the journey from his hut, across the village compound, to the track that led to nowhere.

The matriarch looked at him and nodded her head perceptively, as if recognizing and acknowledging another leader. The chieftain looked at No Hat and Keep Trying as he began speaking to everyone – elephants, tribesmen and even the oxpecker.

"We villagers owe a great debt of thanks to our good friends No Hat and Keep Trying and also to the matriarch," said the chieftain. He turned his head towards her,

"And to the rest of her herd for all that they have done on our behalf. This village and the ground we now stand on is testimony to their very special relationship and ingenuity that made it possible. On behalf of all my villagers, we thank you for all that you have done. Your herd has certainly enriched the lives of us all, particularly that of No Hat. Now travel in peace, in the knowledge you are all welcome back to our village, a village which you helped make possible, anytime – goodbye."

The chieftain raised his spear-come-walking stick, as two tribes women took his arm and gently led him slowly back to his hut, his duty done. Keep Trying conveyed the gist of what the chieftain had said to the matriarch, who nodded tacitly. The villagers also nodded to each other as one was overheard to say,

"His words were absolutely perfect and needed to be said - that's why he's our chieftain!"

The matriarch began to move away. Keep Trying turned and said, "At least I've still got my oxpecker as company!" It was a distraught No Hat who waved continuously until the last of the brown shapes of the herd had completely disappeared, with a new 'tail-end Charlie' bringing up the rear!

No Hat wept unashamedly, making no attempt to hide the floods of tears that now rolled freely down both cheeks. The villagers turned their heads away and moved off, not wanting to add to the boy's unhappiness.

No Hat's mother and father stood either side of their heartbroken son, with their comforting arms around his slumped shoulders. Their gesture of love and understanding was clear for all to see. No Hat's mother kissed him lightly on the cheek, his father ruffled his hair as he whispered,

"Time is a great healer." After a short pause a voice called out, "Anyone for a game of five-aside soccer?" The voice was one of No Hat's friends,

"Yes please," said No Hat bravely, in a suppressed but sobbing voice.

With that, he and his friends ran off to make use of the new football pitch. Within seconds the path to nowhere was completely empty, apart from a considerable number of dung droppings! No Hat's father pointed to the steaming heaps and said,

"Waste not want not," and dashed off for his bucket and shovel.

Some distance away, the chieftain had finally reached his hut.

Meanwhile, further up the track that led to nowhere, the matriarch knew exactly where she was taking her herd. Once the villagers had disappeared from view, Keep Trying was ejected from his temporary promotion in the line. The leader had no intention of allowing Keep Trying to get thoughts above his station. The youngster had been given his due recognition - that was enough.

He was relegated further back in the long file, but not at the rear (age does have its privileges – he was after all, nearly five)! On resuming his rightful place, Keep Trying's mother gave him a gentle caress with her trunk and said how proud she, the matriarch and the entire herd were, of the way in which he had acquitted himself.

Keep Trying waved his trunk in acknowledgement, having lost none of his bounce - time is a great healer.

—∞—

Résumé

Who would have thought so much could have happened to No Hat and Keep Trying in this their second chance encounter, not forgetting of course our faithful friend the oxpecker. To start with, they had only met – like ships that pass in the night - because of the devastating news the dam builders had bought to the village. This had forced No Hat's family and villagers to move far away from the land on which they had lived for countless generations.

Fate and fortune must have formed part of the equation of luck and life - the guardian angels and spirits had not neglected them after all. Not only were No Hat and Keep Trying reunited, it was their brainwave that saved the day and suggested the outrageous plan of using the elephants to move the village – lock, stock and barrel.

Despite the deep-rooted and justifiable doubts of the chieftain, elders and villagers, our two heroes had accomplished the 'impossible'. And just to top it all, Keep Trying had discovered a spring in the nearby foothills – how clever was he?

No Hat was now thirteen-years old, with Keep Trying still to celebrate his fifth birthday. He was such an intelligent elephant he probably did have some sort of party, probably a Thornbush! We're not too sure how old the oxpecker was: he seemed ageless and kept himself in such good condition. They were a trio who had done tremendously well.

Would No Hat ever see Keep Trying again,	the answer was – yes.
Would our two heroes help the stranded animals,	the answer was – yes.
Would our two heroes have further adventures together,	the answer was – yes,
and ones you cannot start to imagine!	
Would any of the ivory poachers get their just desserts,	the answer was – yes.

These are all, however, the subject of a final farewell story, but for the time being:

All's well that ends well

The End

THE ADVENTURES OF NO HAT AND KEEP TRYING

THE FINAL FAREWELL

Robert Villier

Book Three
Trilogy

Contents

Chapter One
Meeting as promised

When No Hat and Keep Trying had bravely bid their last farewells to each other, they promised faithfully that they would do everything within their powers to try and meet up again. However, they both knew that time in the African grasslands was measured only by night following day, and anything could happen, especially if you're an elephant or a boy and not in charge of your herd or tribe.

Only the matriarch knew just how far her herd's radius of operation extended to - many thousands of miles at the very least. But a promise is a promise and neither one wanted to let the other down. To this end, No Hat visited their agreed rendezvous point every single day (well – most days) as the sun went down behind their village, in the hope of seeing Keep Trying there. Days turned into weeks, weeks turned into months and then into years with still no sign of the largest-living-land-animals-on-the-planet.

—∞—

Imagine his excitement then, when almost three years to the day, wonderful grey shapes emerged in the far distance! These majestic animals were slowly returning back down the very same track (that led to nowhere) they had disappeared along thirty-six months previously – who ever doubted elephants never forget? Yet something did not look quite right, something had changed, but No Hat could not quite put his finger on what was different about the returning herd. No matter, it would come to him, and anyway - Keep Trying would explain it all.

As they got nearer, one of the smaller to medium sized elephants broke ranks and came forward at an excited and confident 'bounce' – yes it was indeed Keep Trying! No Hat waved his hat in acknowledgement as the other boys stood nearby, looking on in absolute amazement, as they witnessed this happiest of reunions. Even the herd came to a halt, and some of the older elephants looked across as if they also recognized No Hat. Both had kept their promise, as each had believed they would.

By this time Keep Trying's trunk was now affectionately stroking the top of No Hat's head, and gently wrapping itself around his shoulder like No Hat's father would do with his arm.

It had not gone unnoticed to Keep Trying, that his old friend was sporting a new hat. No Hat reciprocated, and lovingly tugged at a large, happily flapping ear.

It was such an open and genuine show of affection with no attempt to hide each their absolute delight, as they both shouted,

"A promise is a promise." Once the euphoria had lessened, No Hat jumped up onto Keep Trying's back, and Keep Trying turned to him and said,

167

"Welcome back!"

The other boys disappeared, realizing that any involvement they may have had was now overtaken by events — they were resigned to the fact that they wouldn't see much of their friend for the next few days.

The matriarch informed the herd - including Keep Trying — that they would remain in the area for about a week, depending upon the availability of food. This was the signal for Keep Trying to move away with his happy passenger, but not before obtaining permission from his ever loving mother. She had never forgotten the worry and trouble Keep Trying had caused her when he had first got lost — remember the water hole. Since that time Keep Trying had always thoughtfully remembered to ask and tell his mother where he was going.

With No Hat sitting comfortably onboard, Keep Trying started to move away as No Hat remarked,

"This is just like old times."   Then, as if by magic, a familiar looking yellow-billed oxpecker landed behind No Hat on Keep Trying's rump. They both burst out laughing, and Keep Trying dryly remarked,

"Yes – just like old times."

By now the oxpecker was busy scavenging for ticks and had confidently assumed that he was more than welcome – which he was. They both had such a lot to tell each other since No Hat's village had moved. Keep Trying said,

"It's not only good to see you again, but marvellous to be able to have a good old chinwag (*three years apart and out comes a word like chinwag – how does he do it?*). I haven't spoken to anyone since we said goodbye. So you will have to excuse me if at times I tend to go on!" No Hat smiled and shook his head, without doubt Keep Trying was indeed a truly exceptional elephant and he loved him as only a true friend could.

No Hat then joyfully prompted Keep Trying,

"We have lots to tell, you go first," whilst he noticed how much bigger he had grown. Keep Trying went on to explain what an exhausting trek it had been to reach the matriarch's favoured watering hole (after he had left No Hat for the last time). She was by then noticeably looking her age, and the daily walks were becoming more and more laboured, but not once did she ever complain, or let anyone else take the lead, but she *was* becoming painfully slow.

That was until they were chased by ivory hunters, when it had been a frenzied charge into the thick undergrowth and somehow she had managed a short but laboured run. Luckily no one was caught or hurt, but clearly those terrible men were still up to their old evil tricks. Perhaps it was the ivory poacher they had pulled from the pit in their earlier adventures and he had not mended his ways as he had promised to do!

By now most of the villagers had come to see what all the noise and excitement was about. Some of the tribesmen even recognized a number of the elephants who had silently and willingly transported their huts and belongings even though it was a full three years ago, how time had flown. Although the tribesmen never called it a 'year', their calendar of life revolved around the variations in the two predominant seasons: the wet and the dry.

—∞—

By then the herd had spotted a reinvigorated grazing menu of Thornbush, Acacia, Jackalberry trees, Candelabra trees, Whistling Thorn and even their own aptly named Elephant grasses, and had wandered off to enjoy this welcome change in fare. As the herd made their way to their lunch, they passed close by to two distinctly different areas of land.

The first area was No Hat's father's new vegetable plot, which his father had painstakingly dug and continued to weed. He had barely scratched the surface, as it was taking countless hours of strenuous and backbreaking labour.

"Enjoyable work," he had said.

The second area of land was flat, stone-free and well-trodden – the football ground. No Hat explained to Keep Trying that moving their village had been the best thing that could possibly have happened - not that the villagers thought so at the time! No Hat went on to say,

"One village did leave it too late and only left when the water was less than a hundred metres away. So Keep Trying, please will you make sure the matriarch and the rest of the herd know just how deeply the villagers are indebted to them."

Keep Trying patiently waited until No Hat had finished talking and then with his excellent memory, reminded No Hat, that he could distinctly remember meeting the hothead and his villagers, and that the chieftain had already thanked the matriarch and the rest of the herd when they left the last time.

"What poor memories you humans have," he said. No Hat nodded knowingly (he knew he had met his match), saying,

"Yes, now I come to think of it I do remember, I'd forgotten elephants never forget!" No Hat then countered by saying,

"If you will forgive my temporary amnesia, I will take you to the lake. By now it will be deep enough for you to have a good wallow without getting out of your depth, unless of course, you have forgotten how to swim!" Keep Trying laughed and gave him a playful slap with his trunk.

The oxpecker sensed he was again part of a very happy partnership. It had been three full years since the herd had disappeared down the track that led to nowhere, it seemed like only yesterday.

—∞—

Chapter Two
Good and bad news

When No Hat and Keep Trying arrived at the water's edge, they stood for a few moments just looking out at the vast expanse of water which stretched as far as the eye could see (even though elephants had relatively poor eyesight). The many islands looked like ships out at sea, with the tops of a few tall trees still visible in the water.

Keep Trying broke the silence,

"It really is so good to meet up again, but I always thought we would. It seems to have been a long time, especially as we now have three newcomers to the herd; and I am no longer the baby at the back of the lengthening line. By the way No Hat, you look as if you have grown, but you don't feel any heavier," Keep Trying joked.

Just then their immaculate oxpecker re-joined them, he often flew off to stretch his wings or take a comfort break. He didn't stay for long and departed immediately Keep Trying waded into the lake for a refreshing wallow. No Hat sat on the bank, happy and quite content to watch his recently returned friend taking a bath in an exceptionally large pond!

The matriarch still had to discover this rather large watering hole. Eventually Keep Trying clambered ashore and with impeccable timing the pristine yellow-billed oxpecker landed back on to the grey wet moving platform.

Keep Trying then lowered his trunk, almost as a mark of respect, saying,

"I have some very sad news – the old matriarch is no longer with us." No Hat immediately shouted,

"That's what was so different when I saw you all approaching, the grand old lady was not leading the herd." Keep Trying went on to say that,

"The matriarch took us to the site of our ancestor's graveyard. I realized that the visit to this secret ground was very significant, and sensed the spectre of imminent death all around us." *The young elephant had seen the other side of their lives.* Keep Trying said that,

"It was a numbing experience, but I will tell you more when about when the time is right.

No Hat sensed they had both become unintentionally morose and tried to lighten the mood by saying to Keep Trying,

"Tell me all that has happened to you, the new matriarch and the rest of the herd since we last saw each other, and yes, I have been given a new hat." Keep Trying replied light-heartedly,

"Better not lose this one, but you must accept that No Hat you were named and No Hat you will always be!" The words of a unique elephant. Keep Trying then went on to describe the endless and tiresome walks, with little time for fun. The new matriarch was stricter than their dearly departed old leader, but she was much younger. What was that saying: '*A new brush sweeps clean?*'

Jokingly No Hat said,

"Let's get the bad news out of the way first; I'm now back at school, albeit still under a tree." They both knew that he didn't really mean it. It was just that he would much rather spend all his time with No Hat.

The walk to the big tree for lessons was a round trip of ten kilometres, five of which was the average separation between the newly emerging villages that had spread as a ribbon development along the complete length of the range of hills. The daily walk for No Hat kept him 'as fit as a fiddle' (*although he didn't actually know what a fiddle was*).

The school day started at eight and ended at two, so there would be time enough to get back home and enjoy himself with his large grey four-legged friend. The measurements for the new school building had been done – it looked as if the dam builders were going to be as good as their word and would build a new school as they had promised.

The spirits had been kind to the tribesmen. After they had been forced to move off the land which had been their home for many generations, they now found themselves living between a backdrop of gentle folding hills and within a kilometre of a vast lake. Both of these offered new possibilities to these proud and resourceful people — there was no doubting that their ancestral guardians were still looking after them. No Hat went on to explain to Keep Trying how well the village had settled, helped by Keep Trying and the rest of the herd. Without them it would have been a struggle to move as it had been for their neighbouring villagers, who had found it extremely difficult and traumatic.

No Hat's village was the only one that managed to move their huts — thanks to Keep Trying and Co. The other villages had been forced to leave most of their heavier hut poles behind, as they were too cumbersome to lug such a long distance. The livestock had got over their initial shock and excitement of the move and had settled down again into a contented and placid way of life. Needless to say, the cockerels still woke them all up at an unearthly hour of the morning.

No Hat was still waiting to go on his first hunting trip — but more on that later. He then admitted a real liking for his latest pastime — fishing. For the time being, he was just glad to be back with his best ever friend, Keep Trying. This was, by far, the best of the good news. Keep Trying then asked No Hat,

"How is the chieftain? Did he recover from his bumpy ride on my back? He didn't look at all well to me." No Hat was warmed by his friend's enquiry (*not many elephants would have been so thoughtful*). He replied,

"He's really very poorly, we rarely see him. I think the physical effort of the move and probably the worry about it was the start of his decline. The villagers still love and respect him so much and his family are constantly with him. We all go and pay our respects every week, but don't stay long so as not to tire him, but between you and me, it's only a matter of time before he passes away and I think - a short time."

"On a cheerier subject," No Hat said,

"There might be the possibility of us both going on the next hunting party. It will be my first. Apparently I'm still too young to be able to throw a spear with the accuracy and force required, but I can watch and learn, so I've been told. I didn't want to sound ungrateful but I did say that I had a friend with me at the moment. Apparently, the hunting party already know all about you and it seems we might both be invited, so fingers crossed, I don't know what you can cross? It seems that your presence might be a benefit. I can only presume that you may be asked to carry a dead impala, if the hunt is successful."

"Since you left," No Hat continued, "The biggest single event has been the increasing expanse and level of water. The chieftain's siting of our new village could not have been better. As you can see, from the edge of the lake to the centre of the village is no more than half a kilometre."

—∞—

He explained that for bush people the introduction of water was making a profound change to their way of life, and the tribesmen were having to re-educate themselves on this new diverse environment. Also it was having a devastating effect on the animal kingdom. Like the late matriarch, this was a subject which demanded more attention in a later and lengthier conversation.

By then No Hat and Keep Trying had returned to the village. Keep Trying looked by far the greyest elephant, after having had the opportunity to take a dip in the lake. Meanwhile, the herd had drifted off to continue their favourite pastime of eating. Their average intake was over one hundred kilograms of trees, leaves and grasses per elephant per day. The vegetation had grown lush over the intervening years and was ideal grazing for the herd.

Unbeknown to Keep Trying and No Hat this was to be their final swan song together. However, for the time being this thought had not crossed either of their minds and they were living for the moment, content to make the most of their time together. Having again been given permission by their mothers to wander further afield to explore, they set off on their own once more.

The villagers acknowledged them as they passed, no longer completely dumbstruck at seeing them together. The upheaval and traumatic experience of moving the village 'lock, stock and barrel' had greatly altered and widened the understanding of many villagers about elephants.

It now seemed the most natural thing in the world, or at least these grasslands, to see an elephant and a boy going about their daily business, happily talking to each other.

—∞—

Chapter Three
Elephants' graveyard

The next morning our two heroes met up and Keep Trying was keen to explain to No Hat the background and events leading up to the death of their beloved matriarch. The boy listened intently, as he had grown to respect the herd's leader (*from a distance – it has to be said*) and had only heard anecdotes about what actually happened to the largest- living-land-animal-on-the-planet at the end of their life.

Keep Trying set the scene by explaining that there is a legend in Africa that says that the elder elephants know when their death is imminent; and so they leave their herds and travel to a place known as the 'Elephant's Graveyard'. It is believed that this ancestral site has been the final destination of literally thousands of elephants and that their bones and tusks litter the area. However, the graveyard has never been discovered by man, and has been the subject of debate for many years.

Keep Trying went on to say,
"The earlier detour the matriarch had made en route to the promised watering hole had now begun to make sense."

He now appreciated that he was part of a matriarchal society, comprising of so many aunties and family members that he had numerous close bonds within the group. He felt that any death in the family would be a significant event, which impacted on the herd's social structure.

"You can imagine my surprise then, when the matriarch led us all into an area literally covered with hundreds and hundreds of huge skeletal frames, skulls and tusks; this must be the Elephant's Graveyard which we had often heard talked about."

He also confessed that he believed some of the older females thought they recognized some of the skulls and ivory of their own past relatives.

"I suppose because we are so highly intelligent and tactile, it is quite reasonable to assume that we are able to distinguish between our own skulls and those of other species. I must admit I found it quite a chilling experience, but I was glad to see it, all the same. As my mother later reminded me, 'It is all part of the learning curve of growing up. I had cheekily added, 'Being a member of the largest-living-land-animals-on-the-planet', and had got a thick ear," said Keep Trying.

"We must have stayed there for a good hour, during which time the matriarch and a few of the others wandered around, occasionally pausing to stroke a skull lightly with their trunks. I stood almost transfixed as if I was stuck to the spot, looking at the thousands of bones that lay in every direction. It was highly likely that some of my own ancestors lay there somewhere, and it was quite an emotional feeling, although I probably haven't explained myself very well. I was just glad to be left on my own there and was quite relieved when my mother said quietly and almost reverently, 'It's time to leave.'

At this point the matriarch became quite emotional and highly agitated as she came across some particular remains. I could only think that she had been drawn there for some pre-arranged reason. Thankfully, we left shortly after this frenzied outburst; the matriarch was the last to leave and then she turned around for one last look."

Many of the older members of the herd had already remarked that the matriarch had lost a lot of weight, and looked to be suffering from malnutrition. Great rolls of skin now hung limply from her belly, revealing her bones. The give-away was her drive to find water, in the hope of improving her rapidly deteriorating condition.

It is known that elephants that do not improve, develop increasingly low blood sugar, slip into a coma and die. Finally, older elephants whose teeth have worn out (typically after their sixth set) seek out soft water plants and eventually die near watering holes. The final clue was given by Keep Trying's mother who said,

"Be kind and patient with our matriarch, she is not well and may wish to be left on her own from time to time."

On the final visit to the matriarch's favourite watering hole, she seemed to know it. Not only did she spend more time wallowing and spraying, she wandered around the surroundings, as if she was saying goodbye. The rest of the herd did their best to ignore her, pretending that all was well and nothing was amiss.

Did they really fool the sagacious old lady? Elephants normally only sleep about two hours a day (*some say because they are always too busy eating – remember they normally eat for up to sixteen hours every day*).

"Well, most of them must have slept sometime," said Keep Trying,

"Because in the morning after the visit to the watering hole the matriarch had gone!"

They could only surmise that she had slipped away quietly sometime during the night, when the herd was busy either eating or sleeping.

"I'm sure it was the way she would have wanted it to be, no fuss and no need to make unnecessary excuses, opting for a silent and dignified exit." It was the end of a long life, during which she had carried out her duties of matriarch with wisdom, care and total reliability. She had never let them down – ever.

When the herd discovered that she had gone, it converged into a tightly knit group, as if holding a counsel of war. They stood huddled together, waving their trunks high in the air, saluting their departed leader, wherever she may be; at the same time, moving their enormous front feet in a back and forward motion.

They left the matriarch to cope with her death in her own private way. The eldest female who was also the largest, moved to the front of the herd and assumed the mantle of matriarch and the herd moved off.

Keep Trying had concluded that perhaps there was some tacit understanding, which he was too young to understand. When the herd eventually stopped for their long overnight meal, interspersed with the occasional short nap, the new leader approached all thirty-nine members of the herd individually and explained that she would try and follow in the dependable footsteps of her predecessor.

"The old matriarch is dead, long live the new matriarch!" said the herd. The next morning they set off in their customary single file. There was no doubt who the new matriarch was, a grandmother with her daughter and two granddaughters all in the same herd.

Apart from always being in the lead, the matriarch was instantly recognizable by her huge size and her massive ears. Her ears were the size of a door and noticeable for their raggedness, with a number of large chunks missing. She had also lost half of her right tusk. Each was a story in itself. Despite her battled-scarred appearance, the herd were reassured that they were in a new but safe pair of one and a half *tusks!*

The saying that elephants never forget has some backing by science. It seems that it may be particularly true in the case of the matriarchs. Dominant females build up a social memory as they get older, which enables them to recognize friendly faces. They signal whether an outsider is a friend or foe to the rest of the herd, and so allow family members to focus on feeding and breeding when there is no danger.

Sadly, ivory poachers tend to kill the bigger, older elephants, and thereby decrease the survival chances of the whole herd. That said - they've been around for seven million years and hopefully will outlive the poachers.

—∞—

Chapter Four
Hunting party

Early the next morning No Hat was in good spirits (but it would be true to say that both boy and elephant were invariably in good spirits) as he greeted Keep Trying and said,

"I've got three bits of good news for you; firstly, there is no school today; secondly, a hunting party is shortly to leave, and thirdly, you and I have been invited along."

"Well this will certainly be a novel experience for me, we're normally on the receiving end," Keep Trying cheerfully replied, without a trace of rancour.

With No Hat onboard and his spear held firmly across his knees, they set off well in advance of the hunting party, just as the villagers were beginning to stir. The sun had not yet made an appearance, although the cockerels had begun to stretch their wings and exercise their vocal chords. An early start was crucial, as they knew full well that the relentless pace of the hunters would be too much for the best efforts of Keep Trying to keep up with – as best he tried. They say the 'early bird catches the worm', and our oxpecker friend had already taken up his customary position, with no intention of missing any excitement the day may have to offer.

Our heroes had done well, and it was a good hour or more before the chanting of the hunters could be heard, growing louder and louder. No Hat waved to the hunting party, as it overtook them. Keep Trying half-heartedly raised his trunk, accepting defeat as they passed him. The hunters grinned. They wore bright red full-length sarongs, each carrying their own spear and leather shield. Their upper bodies glistened with perspiration from their efforts, but none showed any signs of fatigue as they ran and sang.

They were searching for their favourite prey – the impala, the most common antelope in the whole of Africa. Amazingly, they are one of the very few animals that have increased in number. Today they were looking for the Black Faced Impala, with its handsome features and tender delicate flavoured meat. The males were easily identified by their distinctive thick based horns which curled backwards and upwards, with the tips becoming very shiny with age. The impala are a reddish brown colour, which changes into a paler brown and white halfway down their flanks and onto their bellies, with three unmistakable black stripes on their tail and rear. Impalas live in herds of around twenty and are most active in the morning and evening. They are dependent on water, and never stray far away from it.

—∞—

You may be interested to know that they are the only hoofed animal that engages in reciprocal grooming and are the smallest antelope that is always attended by oxpeckers and tick birds. Keep Trying would also confirm that there were other animals that these birds regularly visited and dined upon, such as elephants. On average an impala weighs about 75 kilograms and is an incredibly agile jumper, often leaping to a height of four metres. Their main predators, not surprisingly, are leopards, cheetah, crocodiles, lions, hyenas, wild dogs and not forgetting – hunting parties!

Eventually the hunting party of five men and three boys of around No Hat's age came upon the impalas. They spread out and advanced at a snail's pace, in hunting mode, after their prey. Their movements were imperceptibly slow, as they remained downwind of them. The slightest hint of movement would be enough for these nervous animals to take flight with their high and majestic leaps.

The skilled hunters, armed only with spears, had to be within a few metres to ensure a deep and telling strike. To achieve such close proximity, the hunters used their shields as a shadow guard, to ensure that no shadow or movement was detectable. No Hat and Keep Trying remained well back as the drama in front of them unfolded. Three of the hunters crouched absolutely motionless for at least twenty minutes (although it seemed a lot longer), still downwind with little likelihood of the hint of any smell being carried to the handsome nostrils of this most graceful looking species. Any movement, whatsoever, would result in them taking flight, as if on wings.

Then a young impala moved within range, and as one, the spears struck home — two of the three spears scoring direct and deep hits. The rest of the herd took off in startled fear, leaving the fatally wounded impala as the prize of the hunters. One of the three hunters carried the spears and shields, whilst the other two carried the dead animal away from life's arena.

However, it was not long before they returned to their grazing. Life went on for the herd of impalas, as it did for all the other groups of animals. The normal procedure after the 'kill' was for the hunting party to rest a while. This was both to recover from the chase and the excitement and theatre of the highly skilled final phase of the hunt. It was a physically and emotionally draining ordeal, and one in which the intended victim had always to be respected.

It also gave them time to regain their strength, before carrying their prize many kilometres home. They did not eat any food, but they all drank a small amount of water, which they carried in small pouches hanging from their waists. They knew that water was more important than food for the long walk home in such a hot temperature.

Today their task was made much lighter because they were blessed with having their own transport. This welcome assistance was without doubt a first for all the hunters and certainly for one of the largest-living-land-animals-on-the- planet.

With No Hat onboard Keep Trying and the impala draped behind him, the hunting party set off back towards the village.

They certainly looked an incongruous sight – the hunters in single file, followed by an elephant and his strange cargo of two - three if you count the oxpecker that had quietly and unassumingly re-joined!

No Hat's spear remained clean and unused, but his day would come. He also learnt that on many occasions no spears found their mark and the hunting party would return empty-handed.

On reaching the village, they received the traditional welcome of a successful hunting party returning home. Presumably someone went out in advance to see if they were triumphant or not? The villagers formed a cheering and clapping avenue, to show their appreciation for a 'job well done.'

The hunters could now relax, the women would prepare a banquet of roast impala – everyone's favourite, except for Keep Trying. He wandered off to join his mother and the rest of the herd to enjoy his own banquet of Jackalberry tree and Acacia.

No Hat, after thanking Keep Trying for his company, returned to the family hut, keen to tell his father how much he had learnt about hunting impala. His father listened attentively heartened by what he had heard, and gave No Hat exactly the encouragement his son wanted to hear,

"I am sure it will not be long before your own spear has been blooded."

During the course of the day the yellow-billed oxpecker (with a blood-red tip on his beak) had noticed his own 'kind' on many of the antelopes and impalas, but decided he preferred the convivial company of No Hat and Keep Trying. In the evening he flew off to his own secret home - either a nest or a hole in a rock wall.

Chapter Five
Passing of a chieftain

The tribe's people woke early the next day to the sad news that the chieftain had passed away peacefully during the night. The euphoria of the successful hunt was instantly forgotten. It would seem that the tremendous strain and upheaval of the last few years had finally taken its toll.

"As a well-spent day brings happy sleep – so life well used brings happy death."

They were all saddened at the passing of their fine leader, but they had to confess that it was not that unexpected. For many months the health of the chieftain had visibly deteriorated, as the engine of life began to splutter and misfire, and the energy tank was running almost on empty. He was, after all, a very old man.

There were no birth certificates in the bush, and no one was older than the chieftain, so it therefore logically followed that no one really knew how old he was – he was just *very* old. Some of the irreverent youngster said 'ancient!'

The chieftain had often recounted stories of his youth when the valley teemed with dangerous animals - he had the scars to prove it! Latterly he had described how the tribes' vast grassland valley had become a sea of water – and crocodiles.

No Hat and other youngsters would sit around his fire, listening entranced to the many yarns he had told many times before and on each occasion there would be some slight embellishment, but the boys knew this. The adults would smile knowingly;

this was a scene they had witnessed hundreds of times before during his illustrious life time.

The chieftain was not bragging and his stories for the most part were true; he had indeed come close to death on more than one occasion. He enjoyed the company, the innocence and enthusiasm of a rapt young audience and his own escapism into history. He would *always* finish his tale by declaring,

"Fellow hunters – my stories are now only memories, but no one can take them away from me! Now all of you – be honest and brave - and leave an old man with his past."

At least the chieftain had the enormous satisfaction of having wisely decided on the move to the new village site. The vast spreading expanse of water was a true testimony to his judgement to move his people. He had successfully seen his village rebuilt and the harmony and satisfaction that had returned to the faces of his beloved villagers. In his heart he knew that he had done the right thing for his people and his duty was complete. It is comforting to know that he probably died a contented man and his hut would remain an empty epitaph to him, and not be washed away by the lake.

—∞—

All activity within the compound came to a complete and abrupt halt. In line with their burial rituals, the tribe turned their undivided attention to honouring their dead chieftain. The women knelt outside his hut, weeping and mourning his loss. The men from all villages queued with their offerings, which they placed reverently into a large wooden bowl, which had been placed at the chief's head. The offerings were personal tokens of special significance to the donor and the chieftain.

The men held a vigil throughout the night, as they mourned the passing of their much loved and admired chieftain. The women brought food and drink for the mourners. In the meantime, other men dug and prepared the gravesite which tradition demanded should not be far from the village. The following morning, his small, still and silent body was taken from his hut and carried on high (wrapped in his favourite blanket) and gently laid in his new resting place – the lovingly prepared grave.

His spear and shield were placed at the empty opening of his hut, as a constant reminder and mark of respect of his remaining spirit. Relatives then called upon their ancestral spirits, naming as many of them as they could remember, asking them to be pleased to welcome their brother into their world. Then, in keeping with tribal customs, at the graveside a goat was killed and a ritualistic meal was eaten. The mourners then bathed, washing away any remnants of death and prepared to continue life normally. This was tribal custom and exactly what he would have wished, showing honour and respect for him in both life and death.

This was one occasion when No Hat remained with his parents and Keep Trying with his herd, as everyone felt the passing of the chieftain. A tangible quietness enveloped the village, and even the cockerels remained silent.

What had to be done was done but without noise and with respectful decorum. By this time, the sad news had spread along the many miles of the range of hills, where dozens and dozens of new villages were springing up. The other villagers had had the difficult task of transporting their huts unaided when they had moved. When they learnt that a herd of elephants had helped one village move, they were genuinely disbelieving and quite flabbergasted. They had all been the victims of destructive visitations by the largest-living-land-animals-on-the-planet. However, they had known the chieftain for many years and he was renowned for being a fine and honourable leader, and they wanted to be part of his final burial ritual.

Many hundreds of tribesmen spent the day travelling to No Hat's village. That night an ox was sacrificed and they all joined in a great feast, with much dancing and

beating of drums. The constant thumping drumbeat was a final salute and 'thank you'
to a chieftain who had led them so well over many years.

Keep Trying watched from afar with the rest of his herd; they were unusually
quiet, as if paying their own marks of respect. His thoughts then returned to the
Elephant Graveyard, thinking,

'Both No Hat and I have lost our leaders. It must be the end of a generation —
we must be the next generation!' These were very profound thoughts for an elephant,
but he was after all an exceptional elephant.

*A spear and shield still lay outside the late chieftain's hut, a hut which the
tribesmen believe still contains two items, one of them clearly visible - his modified
spear-come-walking stick. The second — not seen but strongly felt — was his remaining
spirit.*

—∞—

Chapter Six
In need of boats

The heir apparent was the late chieftain's eldest son. It was a position for which he had been well prepared and educated. The old chieftain had already put in motion the necessary preparatory work for his son to succeed, and to ensure he was comfortable with his new status, as and when the day should come – as it most assuredly would.

The new chieftain was a rather large and jovial married man in his mid-fifties with two teenage daughters, and an equally large and good humoured hardworking wife. They were well-liked throughout the village and beyond; he was a popular choice and his move in to leadership was a seamless transition. Now in charge, the new chieftain made his first decision and statement,

"We must make the encroaching waters our friend, not our foe."

Up until now the tribal people had tried to ignore the growing expanse of water, which was becoming a vast and endless lake. They preferred the familiar and safe havens of the grasslands which had been their historical homelands for generations.

The new chieftain was more pragmatic and accepting of the water than his father. He thought that the way ahead was by using this new environment, and not by fearing it. To this end, he said,

"We urgently need to either beg, borrow, barter or buy boats, to sail, fish or whatever, to take advantage of our changing surroundings." He also raised the question of what to do about all the stranded animals which he knew were vital to their future.

Volunteers were called for, to journey to the new dam, where the river folk had dwelt for years. There they must try to get some boats and learn the rudiments of moving on water. Remember, very few of the tribal people had ever been on water, let alone learnt to swim; No Hat could swim and was one of the few exceptions.

Not surprisingly, Keep Trying and No Hat were the first willing volunteers! By this time, nothing our two heroes did or said surprised the villagers. They now accepted as normal seeing a boy and an elephant talking to each other, even to the point of having differences of opinion. In fact, it was the most natural thing in the world, to see No Hat and Keep Trying together.

The 'boat acquisition party' marvelled as they approached the towering and massive dam wall that now stemmed the flow of the river; the full effect of which was now clear. It stopped the party dead in their tracks, as they stared up in wonder at the concrete structure looming high above them almost touching the sky.

They could see a number of outlets through which large plumes of white water rushed. Was it leaking already? As they got nearer, the dam wall blocked everything else out and filled their field of vision completely.

The top resembled the parapet of a fortress and the people looked like ants or tiny birds. The tribesmen, apart from being staggered by the enormity of its size, simply could not understand how such a gigantic edifice could be built, whilst the river continued to flow.

The river people knew how it was done! They had had a ringside seat over many years, watching how this engineering miracle had been achieved with the use of a 'cofferdam.' The cofferdam was a large "U" shaped concrete and metal construction built out half way across the river.

It had an enclosed area, about half the size of a football pitch, behind the main water-retaining barrier. This enclosed area was then pumped out to create a working environment – a dry enclave - to allow the dam builders to build the foundations and retaining wall. The wall would in turn contain the huge turbines and machinery that would control the flow of water, turning it into hydro-electricity; whilst the river continued to pass through the now narrower channel.

After half the dam had been built, the same procedure was repeated on the other side. It was a huge and demanding civil-engineering project that had taken many years to build. Many dozens of dam workers had fallen to their deaths whilst building it and remained encased forever in tons of concrete.

During this time the river people had had their own lives seriously disrupted, living next door to a building project, which seemed to go on for ever. At least its completion signalled an end to the deafening explosions which had become part of their daily life.

Now with the construction complete, life was returning to a more peaceful existence. That is, apart from having to now contend with the dramatic increase in the number of crocodiles. Their increase in numbers was the result of the formation of the lake, which now provided an ideal habitat for these pre-historic creatures.

The word crocodile was not one the boats acquisition party wanted to hear, especially as would-be novice boatmen. For them, the technicalities of cofferdams were the last thing on their minds. They were more interested in learning how to row their soon to be acquired boats.

Nearby, set back from the river bank, nestled a small village, boasting many boats in different shapes and sizes. The river people were kind, understanding and sympathetic to the boat acquisition party's needs. They offered them refreshments before discussing the purpose of their visit, in a relaxed but business-like manner.

After much good-natured bartering, a deal was done at a fair price, and they all drank a strange alcoholic beverage to seal the arrangement. Everyone had only one drink. The boat acquisition party were mindful of the many moving logs with teeth which flourished underneath the water's surface and all around them; the last thing they wanted was a man overboard!

Eventually both sides were confident of the boat acquisition party's skills, and they left with their newly acquired boats.

—∞—

Chapter Seven
Operation Noah

By the time the boat acquisition party returned home with their two new boats, the tribesmen had become reasonably proficient sailors. The row back across the lake had given them the time to come to terms with being on water. Surprisingly, they had found manoeuvring boats no 'black art', and not nearly as difficult as they thought. They remained cautious of the ever-increasing depth of water, especially as none could swim, and mindful of the many crocodiles!

Keep Trying and No Hat had monitored their progress from the safety of shore, as they made slow passage along the lake. During this time No Hat and Keep Trying could see the islands, large and small, with their inhabitants clearly visible. They had also spotted a number of moving logs with eyes, but it was only the oxpecker who hissed at the crocodiles.

On two of the islands a rhino and a pride of lions were spotted, the first time that No Hat had ever seen these formidable and much-talked about animals. By the time they reached the village the novice boatmen felt reasonably at home on water – if you get my drift?!

Now the tribesmen had to put their newly acquired assets and skills to work. The first attempt to rescue four monkeys ended in complete disaster. The monkeys, by now completely petrified, went straight into an 'attack mode' and badly bit and ripped the skin of their would-be rescuers. A revised plan had more success.

Both boats were used, one manned and one empty. The tribes-come-boatmen threw nets over their unappreciative captives, and loaded them into the empty boat, which they towed back inshore with its noisy and struggling passengers. Releasing the live cargo was fraught with danger, as the monkeys made a rapid dash for freedom, without a single word of thanks!

This simple rescue took an entire morning and saved only four ungrateful 'customers' from one single island, and there were hundreds of islands. Why hadn't the sheer enormity of moving thousands of animals been considered and addressed much sooner? The enormous magnitude of the rescue task soon became evident to all. Clearly this was going to be a mammoth task and not one that No Hat's villagers assisted by the other villages, could do by themselves. It needed a well-equipped team to cope with the huge number of animals in need of rescuing. The chieftain decided to visit the dam builders and request help, after all, this situation was all of their making; and he made his one and only boat journey to the dam wall.

When they got there the dam builder's chieftain, speaking through a tribal interpreter, expressed his condolences at the demise of the late chieftain. News of his death had reached the dam site through either the medium of the 'grasslands grapevine' or the 'bush telegraph.' It had not come from via the chieftain's village. It was a mystery for sure. The dam builder's chieftain smiled ruefully, as he fondly remembered the late chieftain, if only for the hard but fair bargain he drove. He then complimented the tribesmen on their newly acquired nautical skills in becoming tribes-come-boatmen. They had been impressed as they watched the tribesmen manoeuvre their boats alongside the dam's jetty.

They had acquired their 'sea legs' remarkably quickly, although the chieftain couldn't wait to get back on dry land. The dam leader thanked the chieftain for their laudable efforts in rescuing the stranded animals.

"We anticipated the plight of the animals, but we failed. We were too concerned with the political and economic imperatives and got our priorities wrong. However, we have now recruited a team of rescue rangers with motorboats to rescue the animals. They should now be making their first rescue attempt, and they will help you, as and when they can." He admitted,

"They had not given the animals of the valley the due consideration they deserved." The chieftain thanked him for his honesty.

212

The rescue rangers had two large, unattractive but functional, welded metal boats, fitted with powerful outboard engines, and a fast wooden-hulled smaller runabout as a control craft. Initially they used the boats in the area round No Hat's villages to rescue animals from the nearest islands. Approaching an island was not easy, as they had to push through the tangle of half submerged trees poking through the water. The branches snagged boats and clothing, and caused much cursing.

Once the rangers were on the islands they spread large capture nets out across as much of the middle of the island as possible, draping them high over the trees. The rangers, armed with rifles and thunder flashes made as much noise as possible, to drive the terrified animals into the nets. The legs of the trapped animals were then tied together and the animals were gently lifted into the boats, which were covered in the restraining nets. The loaded boats returned inland, stopping short of the shore. Each animal was then lowered over the side and the ties which were holding their legs were released, and the animals dropped into the water.

With the shore so close and the instinct to survive being paramount, the animals usually swam strongly into the shallows and raced off into the surrounding bush. Speed was of the essence, as shock was the greatest risk of death to the animals. The other great danger was our pre-historic amphibians, the many crocodiles had plenty of floating corpses on which to feed, but they still silently patrolled looking for any additional food!

No Hat and Keep Trying witnessed one wonderful survival. After being released one female bushbuck (a small and common antelope) had simply slipped beneath the water, as its energy was totally exhausted. The men quickly pulled the bushbuck to the surface, and brought it ashore, wrapped it in a blanket and placed it near the warmth of the camp fire which they kept constantly lit.

Later that night, No Hat, was sitting around the glowing embers with Keep Trying foraging quite happily nearby, and the oxpecker at an unknown destination. No Hat had time to reflect and remarked astutely,

"It's a funny old world. We always hunted and found impalas near to water, but they will not dare to venture off the island and into the water to swim ashore!

Moreover, I have not yet speared my first impala and here we are trying to save them, with a close relative of the impala family lying beside us, wrapped up in a blanket!" Everyone laughed.

Keep Trying had found the whole turn of events quite bewildering. Although on a number of occasions he did swim out and help tow the boats inshore using his trunk.

Later, the bushbuck staggered to her feet. No Hat, the other villagers and rangers all held their breath, afraid to breathe or move a muscle and watched in silence, as she walked, unsteadily at first, and then more steadily around the circle of men. She walked a full three laps, with the grace possessed by great ballet dancers or beautiful animals, and then turned and disappeared into the night. The following morning Keep Trying pointed out to No Hat,

"You did realize the bushbuck was thanking you all for saving her life!" This gesture from a small bushbuck made the entire operation worthwhile.

Operation Noah had the unexpected benefit of helping the tribes come to terms with the water and using their boats. Their confidence and competence increased with every day they spent on the lake. They soon saw the new environment as a long term bonus and change to their future way of life, although they would always consider themselves to be grassland people, first and foremost. As the chieftain said,

"Make the water a friend not a foe."

Operation Noah lasted six years and over six thousand animals were saved, and either released into the bush or moved to the nearest National Park. Hundreds of snakes were also cautiously rescued - using very long poles and deep sacks!

—∞—

Chapter Eight
Wedding dowry

No sooner had the new chieftain recovered from the shock of his new and elevated position, than his eldest daughter Zalika announced that she wished to be married. He *knew* that she had fallen for someone, but it was evidently sometime *after* the mother and younger daughter Zeshawn had known of the romance! She told him,

"I am in love with a wonderful man!" The man in question was a nineteen-year-old boy named Zareb from the adjoining village.

The news spread like wildfire among the hills. Everyone expected an invitation and looked forward to the festivities and the music. The other young wives were keen to teach the bride-to-be how to become a good wife. They taught her the secret codes and language that would allow her to talk with the other married women, without their husbands understanding what was being said. They explained the ritual and tradition of 'Jumping the broom' which would take place after the wedding ceremony. In this ritual a broom is placed on the floor and the newly married couple jump over it together hand in hand. It is said to symbolize the jump from single life into married life and sweeping away the old and welcoming in the new. Finally, they explained the ritual of drinking from clay pots to denote their union. These and other tribal wedding rituals had remained unchanged over countless generations.

In the next village the groom's father, who was the chieftain, woke up to the realization that he would have to pay a dowry to the family of the bride, and it would be expensive! His only son – Zareb, was going to become the son-in-law of the next village chieftain and any dowry would have to be appropriate for such an honour. In the end a dowry of both a cow and a goat was considered more than generous, and both families were content. This seriously depleted Zareb's families' already limited livestock holding, but he could not let his only son down, nor indeed himself and his wife.

Furthermore, he could not lose face to a village in which there had always been an undercurrent of resentment towards his village and he did not want that. He wanted to ensure that his son was given the best possible start to his married life, as he too had been given by his father.

The chieftain was also astute in realising that here was an opportunity for the two villages to bury the hatchet, for once and for all. The groom's mother had known *long* before the chieftain knew that he would be losing two of his favourite animals!

The excited bride-to-be had been the childhood sweetheart of three years standing to the nervous groom-to-be. In the past their courting had been at, and after school. Now the 'Elephant Spring' that our heroes had discovered, they had a more suitable meeting place. It was nearer to Zalika's village, but that didn't worry the young and athletic Zareb.

His father hoped his son's marriage would heal the fracture that had existed between the two villages for many years. The cause of this fracture had long since been forgotten and it was perpetuated out of rote rather than reason. Perhaps the joining of the two families in marriage and the two Z's – Zalika and Zareb - would bring an end to this silly unnecessary feuding. He decided to speak as chieftain to chieftain, and propose that they all used the wedding broom to sweep away their past differences. They had new villages, so why not a new start?

—∞—

The new chieftain and proud father of the bride-to-be approached No Hat and Keep Trying with a strange and thoughtful request. He knew what a pivotal role the herd of elephants had played in moving his village to their new and safe location; in particular, the journey that his predecessor, the late chieftain, had made on the back of this very same elephant. He, therefore, asked if his daughter could ride to the wedding ceremony onboard Keep Trying, as a mark of the villagers recognition and gratitude to the herd, and with himself and No Hat in attendance. It was difficult to know who was the most delighted – the bride-to-be or Keep Trying!

On the day of the wedding the girls in the village helped to decorate Keep Trying. They adorned the lower part of his legs (by no stretch of the imagination could you call them ankles!) with rings of fresh flowers and placed a large necklace over his head. They draped a large scarlet sarong across his back. No Hat whispered reassuringly,

"Don't worry it's only for a short while, and you look absolutely *great*." In all honesty, Keep Trying didn't look at all worried. The oxpecker, perched in a nearby tree, appeared perplexed, as he had nowhere to sit. Eventually he managed to find a small landing space on the very rear of Keep Trying's back. Whatever was going on, he wanted to be a part of it!

The wedding ceremony was held under the canopy of nature – the sky. The chieftain dressed in full ceremonial garb. He proudly wore his 'badge of office' - a full necklace of lions' teeth - as the lion was the king of the jungle, so the chieftain was head of the village. He lifted his daughter onto Keep Trying and she sat sideways happily on his back, with her father walking on one side and No Hat on the other side (giving Keep Trying a running commentary). They were preceded by a guard of honour of sixteen tribesmen, magnificent in their elaborate feathered headdresses. They wore scarlet sarongs with bands of multi-coloured beads around their necks, wrists and ankles. Each carried a spear and shield; many had found their mark in an impala – but none had ever walked slowly in front of an elephant before!

The bride was dressed in an indigo robe, an elaborate full length kaftan finished in an exquisite blend of colours, complimented by an array of ornate necklaces of many faceted stones. Around her arms, legs and neck she wore copper and brass rings, to symbolize her bond and faithfulness to her husband. A single strand of small white beads had been woven into her hair, giving the appearance of a halo. The visual effect of so many colours was stunning. The four bridesmaids were similarly dressed in Kaftans, but slightly plainer and less intricate in design. The atmosphere of the wedding was enhanced and captured by the ethereal sound of rhythmic drums emanating from distant villages.

The large audience cheered as the happy couple became husband and wife. Everyone cheered as they jumped hand in hand over the broomstick. The chieftain thanked No Hat and Keep Trying for their help and promised that brides arriving onboard elephants would not become a trend for future weddings! No Hat and Keep Trying then moved away, leaving the young married couple to be the main attraction.

The wedding was a joyous occasion, with guests travelling from far afield, some even arriving by boat. Every colour of the rainbow was on dazzling display in some guise or another. The football pitch was the centre stage for the celebrations. A huge bonfire was lit in the centre circle, which provided both light and heat. The food, music and dancing went on until the early hours of the following morning when the bonfire began to die down and the villagers began to make their way home.

The young couple had stepped from childhood to adulthood. Their wedding present from the two villages was a new hut; it was surprise present to help them on their journey of married life. It was built by the men of both villages and any past differences were forgotten, as demonstrated by their combined act of generosity.

By the end of the evening the two chieftains' and their families were sitting happily together. The broom had worked its magic! No Hat led Keep Trying back to his herd, into the relative quiet and darkness, where the herd were grazing contentedly.

No Hat broke off the rings of flowers around Keep Trying and he promptly devoured them. No Hat managed to save the sarong! No Hat thanked Keep Trying for his help and much appreciated contribution to the wedding day.

Chapter Nine
Like minds think alike

The next day, when No Hat went to see Keep Trying, his four-legged friend had significant news to tell him. Keep Trying laid his cards on the table, and explained why he thought that now was the end of their adventuring together. He explained that he was no longer one of the babies of the herd, as since their first meeting there had been a number of new baby elephants. It was also becoming clear that his elder sister was getting itchy feet, and it would not be long before she and the older girls broke away to form their own group.

This would leave Keep Trying alone with his mother for a few more years. He would eventually make the inevitable break and live alone, in common with the practise of most male elephants. It was hard to believe that Keep Trying would eventually live alone, and by choice.

No Hat understood what Keep Trying was saying and realized that he was no longer an immature, playful and irresponsible elephant, but a maturing and sensible member of the largest-living-land-animals-on-the-planet. He said,

"I understand and agree entirely; in fact I was going to say much the same about my own position – obviously we know each other too well." He said that he was now growing into a young man, which behoved him to take his responsibilities more seriously.

His schooling had never been his favourite subject, but he now realized that he must apply himself fully, if he was to make a success of his life. He intended to study hard in the hope of gaining one of the scholarships on offer. He needed to help his father with his new plot of land, which was beginning to bear the fruits of his labour.

At the same time he had taken the new chieftain's advice, and was now spending more time on the water. The village now owned three boats which they were putting to good use on a daily basis. No Hat had become quite an adept fisherman, using a line held lightly across his fingers. From time to time the tribesmen-come-fishermen saw a number of pre-historic predators. On these occasions they returned inshore, rather than risk sharing the lake with the ever-hungry crocodiles. No Hat used his catches as barter in exchange for maize and other crops.

He admitted that he had yet to prove himself with the spear on the hunting forays, but having witnessed at first hand the skills, strength and patience required of a hunter, he knew his time was not yet upon him. They both fondly remembered the bushbuck and the way in which the antelope had expressed her gratitude.

No Hat, the chieftain and most of the elders felt that the dam builders had been as fair and as reasonable as they could possibly have been. They had let the villages and hundreds of tribesmen know when the valley would begin to flood. Admittedly, the tribesmen had not initially been well-disposed to the dam builders, when first told they had to up sticks and move village. The white marker posts the dam builders had staked out - as they had said they would - had proved to be a good location, and was now the place of their new village.

They still had to fulfil their promise to install a fresh water pump, and for their new village a new purpose-built school, with the funded scholarships, but to date they had been as good as their word. Therefore, the new chieftain had no reason to doubt their integrity or pledges. Secretly, the villagers were thrilled at the promise of these unexpected windfalls. They had never been given or offered anything before and would gratefully accept anything of benefit to them.

No Hat's tribe would remember these monumental events in the only way they knew – in song. For these and all the tribal people, music was to their mind what food was to their body. They lived and expressed themselves in rhythm, in their every movement and in song. They would sing and dance whenever they had the slightest excuse or opportunity to lighten a task, or just because they were happy to be alive. They had no written language and their songs became their almanacs and historical records of events. In years to come, the next generation would sing of a talking baby elephant called Keep Trying, and his companion and best friend - a boy named No Hat. They would chant of moving villages, elephants, oxpeckers and rising waters.

Ironically, the dam builders came to the aid of the elephants. From the high towers of the dam wall they witnessed the mercenary ivory poachers slaughtering the elephants and were sickened by these wanton killings. They dashed to the nearest township and alerted the local constabulary of the horrors they had seen. The police quickly arrived and apprehended the ivory poachers. One of the men arrested wore a red and white bandana with a large gold earring and a scarred face. This was the ivory poacher No Hat and Keep Trying had rescued from the pit in their earlier adventures together! The removal of one band of ivory hunters would not solve the problem, but it was a start and a deterrent to other terrible ivory poachers.

All good things must come to an end, and both Keep Trying and No Hat had inwardly, and secretly, been thinking to themselves, perhaps now is the right time to 'call it a day' – but how could they do this without hurting the other's feelings? In the end the matriarch decided for them. She informed the herd they would not be returning, and now was as good a time as ever to move on whilst the imminent threat and fear of ivory poachers had been removed – certainly for the time being. Keep Trying told No Hat of the matriarch's intention and both nodded and shouted out together,

'Great minds think alike.'

—∞—

Chapter Ten
All's well that ends well

The new matriarch was a stickler for punctuality.   When the time of the next move had been decided upon, she expected the herd to be formed and ready to move off. It was done with an almost military preciseness. She planned the departure for later that same afternoon, when the sun had lost most of its heat; far better to walk in the cool and shade of the evening.

The majority of the day would find the herd eating, stocking up for next of many long walks that would follow. This left Keep Trying and No Hat with only a few hours left together. When they met up, Keep Trying told No Hat of the herd's planned ETD - Estimated Time of Departure, and felt that today's leaving was the right time for both of them to say a last goodbye and a final farewell.

With No Hat sitting comfortably onboard Keep Trying, and the eavesdropping oxpecker in close attendance, they wandered off to share their last few hours of privacy together. They both knew that this was the last time that they would be enjoying the pleasure of each other's company. Without saying a word, they had both thought to themselves, 'Better we stay cheerful and enjoy our last few precious moments together, rather than being downcast and miserable, which would not help at all! No Hat then broke the silence by saying,

"I hope you don't mind my asking, but something has been puzzling me for a very long time, so would you mind if I asked you a very personal question?"

"Not at all," replied Keep Trying, "Surely we know each other well enough by now not to feel embarrassed by answering any awkward questions."

"Well you've got three toenails on your hind feet and four toenails on your front feet, is there something wrong with one of your feet?" said No Hat boldly. Keep Trying laughed saying,

"Yes, I also thought I was unique at first, but having checked every elephant in the herd, it appears that we are all the same."

"Well you are unique, how many other elephants do you know that can *talk!*"

"Now it's my turn," said Keep Trying.

"Fire away," replied No Hat.

"You know how frightened you were when we crossed the river, which I know, was made all the more scary, because you couldn't swim. Well - did you ever get round to learning?" No Hat hesitated before answering:

"Well yes - after a fashion. I am self-taught, along with two other friends who also wanted to learn how to swim. As the lake got deeper we would wade out until the water level reached our waist, and then strike out for the shore. It was always reassuring to be able to put my feet back on firm ground. It is all a matter of confidence, but yes, I can now swim, but only marginally better than my spear throwing!"

No Hat went on to say,

"I still remember and admire the way you slipped into the river, without ever having been out of your depth before - *that* took real courage. You were marvellous." They both laughed, completely at ease in each other's company. So much had happened since their first attempt to recover No Hat's elusive straw hat, and the weird names they had given to each other. Funnily enough, the names had stuck, and no one now thought they were strange names at all.

They had learnt a lot and experienced a great deal. It had been great fun and a unique partnership that was sadly coming to an end.

—∞—

Later that afternoon, the herd wandered up to the edge of the village, with the matriarch looking every bit the leader that she was. Her massive and badly tattered ears looked like two old weather-beaten sails. The end of her broken tusk was the size of a dinner plate. These scars only served to enhance the picture of a magnificent elephant, which had experienced and survived whatever nature had thrown at her.

The entire village community of ninety people, all shapes, sizes and ages gathered to witness the herd's final farewell. Only one sixteen-year-old boy, wearing a battered straw hat stood conspicuously apart from the rest.

Elephants were highly intelligent animals, of that there was no doubt, and their appearance together in front of the tribe was almost a formal gesture of a final farewell. The villagers sensed the significance of this sombre but majestic display and wanted to share in the last few moments of such an occasion. Each member of the village had their own personal memory of how the herd of elephants had helped shape their lives as a result of the three day trek to move the village and then their time together setting up the new village. Over time they had come to recognize many of the individual members of the herd. In return the elephants looked back at them in clear recognition, either waving their trunks, flapping their ears or moving their front feet backwards and forwards at them, or a combination of both.

Save for the private thoughts and the palpable ambience of the village and surrounding African savannah, not a single word was spoken - this was not a time for words.

There were no tears from No Hat – a promise is a promise, and he bravely fought to keep his word. Their days of adventuring together were over, with no regrets, just lots of very happy and special memories, which they would both always cherish. His understanding father gave him a strong reassuring hug, and his loving and equally understanding mother gave him a gentle kiss on the cheek (which did feel slightly damp, if not wet) and whispered,

"Time is a great healer." No Hat pointed with his beloved hat to the heaps of steaming dung, and with a brave and heavy heart, and a large lump in his throat, pluckily said,

"Waste not want not!"

Keep Trying briefly reared up on his hind legs, supported by two feet which boasted only three toenails on each. He held his trunk high in the air and roared, as only an elephant can.

He then shook No Hat's hand *(using his trunk – of course)* for one last time and said,

"I wonder whatever became of that little oxpecker that has travelled with us since we first met?" At that very moment a very familiar looking yellow-billed oxpecker landed on Keep Trying's back! All but one person laughed.

The matriarch then moved off, followed slowly by the rest of the herd, which had formed into their customary single file. The herd's next stop would be much sooner than they thought. It would be an unexpected and pleasant surprise, a detour to enjoy a dip in the lake at the spot previously visited by No Hat and Keep Trying and entirely based on Keep Trying's recommendation.

This brief dip would be much appreciated by the herd before they then set off on the next of many long walks. They left behind their unmistakable calling cards – heaps of steaming dung which were good for the soil – and there were plenty of both! No Hat's father would make good use of it all (waste not want not).

Keep Trying waited until the very last moment and then moved ahead of the new tail end Charlie, who was bringing up the rear, and last of the largest-living-land-animals-on-the-planet. Keep Trying turned around one last time and winked at No Hat and then disappeared from view for ever.

No Hat stood for a full five minutes alone with his thoughts and memories, staring at the empty track that led to nowhere.

The final résumé

That was the end of No Hat's and Keep Trying's adventures together. It had been a unique partnership and a strange alliance that had been forged between a baby elephant and a young African boy, made all the more incredible by their being able to communicate and understand each other perfectly, and get on so well. If you had told anyone what No Hat and Keep Trying and the oxpecker had got up to over seven years they simply would not believe you. But as you now well know, it was all unbelievably true.

To think it all started with our two heroes getting lost, a straw hat and the mischief making of Lady Luck. Not only did they have exciting and scary times together, it brought out qualities in them which they didn't know they possessed. The care and consideration they displayed to others was something most villagers affectionately remembered them by. It was a friendship that enriched both of their lives, and pleasingly benefitted the lives of so many others – both human and animal. No Hat would sometimes look out at the vast lake and think to himself, 'We used to live under there!'

Not surprisingly, Keep Trying was never again able to use his talking ability and it remained his secret throughout a long and happy life. He eventually left his mother, the matriarch, and the herd, to go and live alone — by choice. The elephants had a happy ending; the matriarch led her herd many hundreds of miles away, and they were never again troubled by ivory poachers.

In later life No Hat would recount to his own children the story of the time he shared with a talking elephant. He studied hard and was awarded a scholarship, securing a good job working in the township whilst still living in the village. It was the best of both worlds — the city and the savannah. The third member of the famous three - the yellow-billed oxpecker with the red tip on the end of its beak, was often seen on other animals.

All's well that ends well

The End

Lightning Source UK Ltd.
Milton Keynes UK
UKOW07f0416040315

247255UK00007B/95/P